# Obedience:
## IS IT
# WORTH IT?

*A Journey Through Divorce and
God's Restoration on the Other Side*

# WILMA LORMIS

## Dedication

To my daughters, Reba and Libby, who shared this unwanted journey and gave me increased motivation to strive to be an example in everything I did. Your counsel (often unknown to you and sometimes unwanted by me) helped steer our morphing family into what it is today. I love you both with all of my heart and thank God for giving you to me as daughters.

To my sister, Sandy, whose willingness to read, critique and edit this book, several times without complaint, serves to demonstrate the kind of person you are. Throughout my life you have always been my biggest cheerleader and I'm truly grateful to God for you.

To my husband, Chuck, who began telling people I was writing a book before I ever really started. ☺ Without your encouragement, this book would not yet be a reality. Your belief in me, and the story I have to tell, encouraged my every step. You truly are my surprise package from Jesus!

And lastly, to those who continue to stay in a challenging marriage, are fighting for a seemingly hopeless one or have recently been released from the pursuit. God knows. He sees. May His grace sustain you, His Word guide you and His peace restore your soul. And, for whatever it's worth, I'm cheering you on!

# TABLE OF CONTENTS

# INTRODUCTION

*"The journey of a thousand miles begins with one step."*
*Lao Tzu*

Obedience: Is it worth it? Over the years I have asked myself this very question a multitude of times and in a variety of circumstances. But the hardest, and most likely, longest season of choosing to go against the desires of my flesh and walk in surrendered obedience to Jesus Christ was during the period leading up to, during, and after my divorce... until my husband remarried. Though it was not a perfect walk, it was a determined one. Filled with purpose and intent. And pain. And joy. And tears. And laughter. And brokenness. And, eventually, on the other side of it all, wholeness once again. A process that, for me, took years.

Written in this book is my personal journey, along with a number of things I gleaned along the way. Within these pages, to the best of my ability, I have attempted to include a glimpse of the personal struggle of choosing to obey what I believed Jesus spoke to my heart during that season. Even when those around me, some of whom I deeply respected and trusted, disagreed with me or encouraged me to simply move on.

I will be the first to confess that my journey was not a perfect one. (And still isn't today!) That is why I am so thankful for a loving Savior whose grace is more than enough, when I am not. In the pages of this book you will see some of the good, the bad and the ugly that lies within me. I'm not proud of any of it. Truth be told, any good that lies within me is because of Christ and what He has done in my life. For that I am truly humbled and grateful. In reality, the struggle between right and wrong is a daily battle, providing each of us opportunities to choose which path we will follow. For those who have walked the painful journey of betrayal and broken relationship, in any form, it may be easier to understand, as I do, that this struggle is not unique to any one person. It is humankind, the age-old struggle in every one of us between right and wrong, good and evil. It is fallen man and the struggle that causes one to choose between continued transformation into the image of a loving Savior or falling prey to the wiles of the enemy of our soul.

In the Bible, Romans 7:14-15, 18b-25 (NIV), the Apostle Paul described it this way:

> We know that the law is spiritual; but I am unspiritual, sold as a slave to sin. I do not understand what I do. For what I want to do I do not do, but what I hate I do… For I have the desire to do what is good, but I cannot carry it out. For I do not do the good I want to do, but the evil I do not want to do—this I keep on doing. Now if I do what I do not want to do, it is no longer I who do it, but it is sin living in me that does it. So I find this law at work: Although I want to do good, evil is right there with me. For in my inner being I delight in God's law; but I see another law at work in me, waging war against the law of my mind and making me a prisoner of the law of sin at work within me. What a wretched man I am! Who will rescue me from this body that is subject to death? Thanks be to God, who delivers me through Jesus Christ our Lord!

So, I invite you to journey with me. And as you do, I hope you will hear the gentle voice of the Holy Spirit through these pages, encouraging and guiding you right where you are. And together we will grapple with the question and cost of obedience, exploring what that meant for me. And if you are willing, what it may mean for you.

Your friend and fellow sojourner,
Wilma

## Chapter One

---

# HOW IT ALL BEGAN

*"When you realize you want to spend the rest of your life with some-body, you want the rest of your life to start as soon as possible."*
*—When Harry Met Sally*

**"DID YOU SEE** that new guy?" One of my girlfriends quietly whispered to me as we huddled together talking.

"Yeah." I smiled and asked, "You mean the 'tall' one, right?" Knowing that she knew I had a height requirement for any potential spouse.

We both chucked as she nodded yes.

I met my husband the first year in Bible college. Both of us were involved in the same extracurricular missions group that travelled on weekends, conducting mission services in different churches. Two and half years later, the summer before our senior year in college, we tied the knot.

Both of us had grown up in divorced homes, so prior to our marriage we agreed that the word divorce would never be part of our vocabulary as it related to our family and marriage. We both understood the pain, turmoil and devastation that come from the wake of a divorce. And, of course, we *never* wanted that for *us*!

In reality, most people don't get married thinking, "My end goal is divorce." And if there is someone out there who thinks that, that certainly would not be the norm. Most of us believe that we will live *happily ever after!* After all, isn't that what the movies tell us??

For the most part, we did live happily ever after. Well, for 15 years anyway. That's not to say we didn't have our share of normal challenges and struggles from time to time. Overall, however, we did have what most (myself included!) would have considered a good marriage. By year 15 we had two wonderful daughters, ages 12 and 10, and had been serving as missionaries on African soil for 7 years, which had been one of our long-term goals, even before marriage. Life was good!

*LITTLE CHOICES.* "Catch the foxes for us, the little foxes that are ruining the vineyards." Song of Solomon 2:15

We had become like most married couples after 15 years - comfortable with life, each other, and, more than likely, taking each other for granted…at least to some extent. We were busy with our normal: daily commuting the girls to school, church planting, teaching at the Bible school, as well as various other demands of ministry.

To be very honest with you, I'm really not sure exactly when it was that things began to go south. I do know that I began to notice changes in attitude, tenderness, our sex life, communication, and our overall general rhythm of life. They were barely noticeable at first. You know, when you ask yourself, "Is something wrong here?" but then you quickly dismiss it as an overactive imagination. After some time, on more than one occasion, I asked my husband if he sensed anything different in our relationship or if something was wrong, to which he simply replied, "No."

At first, I believed him and chalked it up as me being overly concerned; by now we'd been married more than 16 years and he'd never given me reason to doubt his word, his actions or his integrity. However, try as I might, I just couldn't shake that little nagging voice inside of me saying, "Something's wrong."

As time went by, I became more convinced that there really was something going on beneath the surface, but I wasn't sure what. On more than one occasion I asked my husband what was wrong and what we might do to try and fix it. Nonetheless, this slow, dull erosion of our marriage, of which I could not get ahold of no matter how hard I tried, continued to slip right through my fingers. When the gentle approach didn't work, I tried a more confrontational approach, asking some very pointed questions, hoping this may break through the wall that was now palpable between us. No matter the question, the response remained unchanged: "Nothing was wrong." I suggested finding someone to talk to or marriage counseling, among other things. Whatever it was, I now knew it was there, and I was making no ground on finding out what it was or a way to work through it. Sadly, over time, those small cracks became huge chasms that I couldn't seem to cross no matter how hard I tried.

I remember one time, waking up in the middle of the night to find my husband was not in bed. I slipped my robe on and stumbled through the darkness into our living room where he was watching a VHS movie. He quickly shut it off. I asked what he was watching. "Nothing," he replied. I asked him to turn it back on so I could see what he had been watching. After a few words back and forth, he reluctantly turned it back on. It was an R-rated movie with nudity that should have never been brought into our home. When I asked why he was watching a movie like this and where he had gotten it, he told me he had 'borrowed' it from someone. I told him I felt it was inappropriate for him to be watching that kind of movie. He proceeded to tell me there was nothing wrong with it and I was just being overly conservative. I asked him, "If there is nothing wrong with this, why did you shut it off so quickly? And why are you trying to hide it from me?" A few more words were exchanged. I slid back in bed, alone, and prayed and cried out to Jesus. There was something definitely wrong and this had confirmed that it wasn't totally in my mind.

I began to look for more evidence in our home, wondering what else I might find. I did come across five or six more of these types of movies hidden in a box. I confronted him on these as well, to which he responded that I was just being prudish.

During this time of ambiguity, a myriad of emotions visited me. Anger. Sorrow. Depression. Fear. Pity. Jealousy. Love. Dejection. Shame. Determination. Weariness. Anxiety. You name it, I probably felt it at some point in this unwanted journey. Some emotions stayed awhile. Others would leave and then come back with a vengeance. Still others seemed to cycle through like the clothes going through their sequence in a washing machine.

There were times the enemy would say things like something was wrong with me or that I couldn't satisfy my husband and that is why he had to look elsewhere. I examined my own heart before God to see if there was any truth to these thoughts vying for my attention. On a good day, I knew in my heart they were not true. I realized I needed to fight these thoughts with truth from God's Word and the reality of the situation. The truth was that my husband was making choices I could not control and they were not my fault. I asked God to convict him and bring him to a place where he would be honest with himself, and then together we could resolve to fight for our marriage, whatever the underlying issues. That, on most days, is what I truly desired…our love and marriage back. Even though I prayed, it seemed as though my prayers were hitting the ceiling and bouncing right back on my head.

I've never been one to put my head in the sand, so I began to ask God to give me wisdom in moving forward, to show me what was there and how to navigate through it. It was at this point I spoke with a missionary friend who was with a different denomination. Through the years she had become a very dear friend, prayer warrior and confidant. I shared with her my concerns and my suspicions, the deterioration of our marriage and asked her to join with me in asking God to bring truth to light. We prayed. Together we were asking God to reveal what was at the root of our disintegrating marriage.

OBEDIENCE: IS IT WORTH IT?

You know how some scenes from life are etched in your mind? I remember quite vividly the moment different realities began to surface and things began to converge. It was clear that something was going to come to a head in the not too distant future.

It was the Christmas season of 2000. My girls were back from boarding school. A missionary colleague and I had taken our kids to do some Christmas shopping at one of the newer "malls" in the city where we lived. Even though things appeared to be festive and Christmassy, I couldn't help but wonder when this cauldron bubbling beneath the surface would blow. While the kids were walking around together, I sat down with my colleague. She and her husband had become dear friends. I remember thanking God for giving me such good friends, ones that become like your family on the mission field. I knew she and her husband were bound to have noticed some of the behavioral changes in my husband since we'd worked closely together for several years. I was confident she just might be able to shed light on some of the things I'd been wondering about.

Sitting on the bench, with nothing to lose, I took a deep breath and then asked her a question that had been rolling around in my head for quite some time. "Is my husband having an affair?" I was quite sure my question had caught her off guard. Her response, with tears in her eyes, jolted my senses and confirmed what I had suspected all along. "Wait until after Christmas and I will tell you everything I know." You see, she deeply cared for us and wanted my girls to have at least a semblance of a 'normal' Christmas before what seemed inevitable would happen. The emotional, life-impacting tsunami would soon hit and forever alter our family as we then knew it.

A few days after my conversation at the mall, I met with her and her husband. I talked them into telling me what they knew so I could be prepared when the meeting to expose truth took place. I assured them I would wait until after Christmas to deal with any of this so at least Christmas could be normal. I learned that the national leadership had had a meeting with my husband, confronting him with accusations of things they had heard from believers in the various churches. It seemed my suspicions were proving to be true. I drove and met with another very dear couple that I had come to love and respect during our years here. The husband was one of the national leaders within our denomination. He was a quiet, soft-spoken man who was well respected. I asked if he would be willing to call a meeting with my husband, our fellow missionaries, the national leadership and me; so they could, once again, present the various allegations to my husband with me being present. Then my husband could no longer hide things from me and we could be free to try and work through the real issues affecting our marriage. At first, he declined, reiterating that the national leadership had already spoken with him about these. I knew what I was asking of him was a very difficult thing. You see, in many cultures, Madagascar included, people are not comfortable with direct confrontation and are very much concerned with the ability for one to save face. Don't misunderstand me, they do deal with things and certainly get their points across; however, it usually comes through a more indirect, storytelling approach.

I explained to him how American culture is different, how my husband had been denying that anything was wrong with our relationship and why I felt I needed to be there when they confronted him again on the allegations. If each of the leaders shared what they knew, truth could be established. I further explained that my desire was that through the confrontation of truth from men who loved him, this would, hopefully, cause him to acknowledge what had happened and repent. I knew that without acknowledging what he had been doing, accepting responsibility for those actions and some form of repentance, there could be no working on our marriage. Reluctantly, my gracious, godly African friend and colleague agreed to call the meeting, the day after Christmas, with the other leadership in attendance. Together they would confront my husband a second time. However, this time I would be present and could ask questions that would, hopefully, bring about more truth, which could serve to bring the situation to a head, and ultimately some kind of healing to our fractured relationship.

Prior to Christmas, I continued to gather more information for that meeting which could help me navigate the impending storm that would inevitably hit on December 26th. Even though this storm remained most unwelcome and unwanted, I knew it would at least serve to help bring truth to light, giving us a chance to begin rebuilding… whatever that might look like. In the midst of suspicions being confirmed and internal chaos trying to overwhelm me, God was there. I was amazed at His goodness in the midst of the impending squall. To my astonishment, God had gone ahead of us and brought in additional emotional support through friends who were scheduled months ahead of time to be the speakers for our upcoming missionary retreat. I had no idea how welcomed and needed these friends would be during this time. I stood in awe at His goodness to all of us, in spite of the storm. Or maybe it was because of the storm?

Christmas arrived. And that evening so did our friends. To be honest, I don't remember much of the day except that awkwardness and superficiality seemed to scream at me from every corner. I wondered if anyone else felt it? I hoped our girls didn't. I wanted to shield them from the impending storm, but I knew I couldn't. I simply lifted up a prayer to my heavenly Father, asking Him to carry them safely through it. I remember asking Him, too, to redeem our marriage and to work in both my husband's life and mine to bring good out of this awful situation we found ourselves in. I was curious as to whether our friends from the States sensed the tension when they arrived in our home. Up to this point they were not aware of anything that was going on. Thankfully, some time that evening, I managed to find a moment alone with our friends and warn them briefly about what was going to take place in the next 24 hours. I hoped it would at least give them a few moments to spiritually and emotionally prepare for whatever was coming our way.

My new vantage point, confirming betrayal, only served to increase my anger and pain. Yet somehow, by the grace of God, my sincere desire was to give God the seemingly impossible opportunity of redeeming our marriage. I reminded myself of the scripture, "Is anything too hard for the Lord?" (Genesis 18:14a) At that moment I hoped and prayed it was true.

## Chapter Two

---

# THE BIG BANG

*"It's easier to forgive an enemy than it is a friend."*
*William Blake*

*"For there to be betrayal, there would have to have been trust first."*
*Suzanne Collins*

EVEN THOUGH I had grown up in the Midwest, I never missed the snow at Christmastime. Rather, I enjoyed the balmy weather and the opportunity to go for a swim on Christmas day if we desired. However, this particular day didn't feel like the day after Christmas. Even though the weather was typical for a summer's day in sunny Africa, complete with a beautiful blue sky, my spirit felt heavy, dark and cold. So many emotions clamored for my attention that I'm not really sure what I felt. A numbness seemed to consume me as I watched the proverbial unwanted clouds of this huge impending tempest roll in, knowing that in a very short time it would relentlessly beat and batter the doors of my home. Worse yet, my family. I remember thanking God for His mercy in allowing the meeting to be scheduled first thing in the morning and or the gift of bringing our seasoned pastor friends in from the States or this very moment. His mercies truly are new every morning!

That day, the drive to meet with our Malagasy leaders seemed to last forever. In reality, it was only about thirty minutes. The tension in our 4x4 truck was palpable, and the conversation between us was all but non-existent, except for the occasional repetitive question from my husband. "Do you know why the leadership has asked us to come for a meeting today?" he asked. "I'm not exactly sure…", I replied, as I choked out my response, hearing my own voice trail off. I began to focus on the thoughts that were swirling around in my head. "How would these impending realities affect us? How would it impact our family? The national Church? Our friends? Our ministry? Our ministry partners?" The questions continued to batter against my frail emotions. My stomach joined in the action, churning and in knots. I wanted to throw up. At this particular moment, even though I had initiated the meeting, I wanted to run away from what was about to happen. "Oh God," I prayed, "Help us all get through this. Please bring truth to light and redeem our marriage from this whole, ugly situation."

The meeting began. So did the accusations and accompanying denials. He had been seen with another woman by different church members and pastors in a variety of settings. It seemed like we were making no headway at all. Nonetheless, I felt like I had a better understanding of what had been happening behind the scenes, things I had only sensed, but was never able to confirm. None of it pleasant, but necessary to know the reality with which we were dealing. The more issues that were skirted and denied the more my anger rose. I breathed a silent prayer, "God can you help me with this anger?" I knew in my heart that God could work and redeem any situation. And I hoped against all odds that this one was no exception.

I don't remember exactly how everything played out in that meeting, but I do know the ending wasn't pretty. I was angry, hurt and felt even more betrayed because of my husband's continued refusal to admit any wrongdoing. He ended up driving our 4x4 truck back to our home by himself and I took a taxi. I needed some time alone, to regroup and to think. To pray and attempt to collect my thoughts. How could he sit there and deny every one of those allegations? How could he refute so many different scenarios and situations? Surely what I was sensing was not in my head and the changes in his behavior toward me only served to confirm these allegations. And the accusations came from too many different sources to be made up. What do I do now? What do I tell the girls? What was going to happen? A myriad of unanswered questions and emotions swirled around inside of me.

As the taxi got closer to our home, amidst the many feelings and emotions, again, I thanked God for my African brothers who were willing to put aside their own comfort to help us deal with this in a way that could possibly bring truth and healing. His faithful provision of our friends arriving less than 24 hours ago was also something for which I could be grateful. I gave a big sigh. I was truly thankful they would be at the house when I got home. I couldn't imagine entering it now without them being there.

Months earlier, when we had invited them to come be our speakers for our missionary gathering, none of us, except God, knew what their real ministry would be during their time with us. They would minister to our family and our missionary team, helping each of us deal with the pain and realities of the present situation. Certainly nothing any of us had wanted or envisioned for this time. And God, in His faithfulness, had provided what was needed for this very moment long before we knew this day would come.

The next several days were a blur. Tension was high in our home and at our fellowship meetings, which were supposed to be a 'retreat.' I became even more grateful for the couple Jesus had graciously sent to our home to serve as a buffer. On January 1st, it was time for our girls to return to boarding school. I accompanied our girls on their flight to Nairobi, Kenya, and then the hour and 15-minute drive to their boarding school. It seemed logical, at the time, to allow them to go back to school to finish out the year. I hoped this could possibly shelter them from some of the storm, providing them a safe and secure environment where they were loved and well taken care of as they continued school. I also hoped that it would give my husband and me time to go back to the States, get some intensive counseling, and try to figure out how things fell apart and where we could begin the arduous work of rebuilding. In my mind, rebuilding was our only choice. Divorce was not an option.

The same day my flight returned to Madagascar, my husband was on a plane heading back to the States. He had been instructed to go directly to a counseling center in Ohio, which was prepared to provide help for us. I stayed back another 5 days, packing a few of our belongings and sorting the rest to sell. I was aware of situations like ours and knew, under the best-case scenario, the earliest we could be back serving again as missionaries was a minimum of two years - an outcome that depended totally on us. I knew that if we both allowed Him to, God could rebuild trust, relationship and bring healing. Oddly enough, though shattered, I now had a better idea of what we were dealing with as a couple and was hopeful that God could redeem our marriage. And I was honestly ready to work hard to allow Him to do that.

I was truly grateful for the missionaries and Malagasy pastors' wives that rallied around me and helped with the daunting task of sorting through all of our things. The majority would be put aside to sell. I would pack a few things to bring with me. In only four days our home was mostly sorted out. During that time, I had heard from the boarding school. Somehow the girls' father had contacted them and told them they would be coming to the States at this time, which only added to their confusion. In light of everything, the girls were having a hard time settling back in at boarding school. In the end, the girls and I decided that we would come back to the States together and not wait until semester's end to finish the school year.

So, on January 10th, I boarded a plane heading to the States via Kenya. With a heavy heart, I slowly buckled the seatbelt on the plane, fighting back tears, as I looked out the window and sighed with a heavy heart. Would I ever have the joy and privilege of ministering in this country again? Not only had this been a fatal blow to our family, but the loss of the people and the ministry that had become so very dear to us during the past 9 years seemed almost too hard to bear.

With only 2 days scheduled in Kenya, the time flew by like a whirlwind. After more packing, tying up loose ends and quick goodbyes, the girls and I headed to the Jomo Kenyatta International Airport in Nairobi. Like it or not, we were bound for the USA, with all of our worldly possessions whittled down to two suitcases each.

Normally, a trip like this carried with it some sadness of temporarily leaving our country of calling, but mostly lots of excitement in anticipation of reconnecting with family, friends and the many partners who enabled us to do our work in Africa. This journey, however, was different. We didn't know how long we would be in the States or how long it would be until we returned to the country of our calling, if ever. We were heading to a place in Ohio that provides intensive counseling to pastors, missionaries, and their families who have gone through various trials and traumas. I tried to present as positive of a front as possible for my daughters, encouraging them, and myself. I reminded all three of us that God could do anything and He would be faithful to see us through no matter what mountains lie ahead of us. We only had to trust God and rely on Him to help us, following His leading along the way. However, at my core, I knew the reality was we were in for a long, hard journey ahead. Little did I know just how long and how hard this journey would prove to be.

# Chapter Three

---

# FINDING EQUILIBRIUM

*"One of the hardest lessons in life is letting go. Whether it's guilt, anger, love, loss or betrayal. Change is never easy. We fight to hold on and we fight to let go."*
*Mareez Reyes*

NOW BACK IN the States, I found myself appreciative for God's provision yet again. The girls and I found ourselves in a fully furnished, simple apartment, thanks to the counseling center and the generosity of others who provided these for families in crisis. After a jetlagged night's sleep, each of us began counseling right away. Over the next few days, not wanting the girls to fall behind academically, I enrolled them in a nearby Christian school and got what was needed for them to begin. In just a few days they were back in school. Not long after that, my husband came.

After only a week at the counseling center, and having attended 2 or 3 counseling sessions, my husband said he "can't sit around here and do nothing for 6 months" and that he prayed about it and "God has released him and told him to go and change careers." I thought to myself, "I'm not sure what 'god' told you that, but I'm quite sure that is not what I am hearing." After picking up the girls from school and bringing them back to our apartment, he said goodbye and left to go back to his hometown. The girls and I were devastated and confused. Although I tried not to show it to the girls, I was furious too. "Good!" I thought to myself, "Go ahead and go! Take the easy way out. You want to do your own thing, go ahead! The girls and I will be better off without you! I'll make a place for the girls and me. I'll make a home for us. Somehow, we will make it." Heartbroken, angry, and not a few tears later, I found myself trying to wade through innumerable emotions and figure out what was best for the girls and me and what to do next. We stayed at the counseling center for a few more weeks, trying to work through as much of the pain, confusion and trauma these past few weeks, well, in actuality, last few years, had produced.

During the girls and my time at the counseling center, I emailed my husband several times, apologizing for any part I had played in this and expressing my desire to work on our marriage, to get to the heart of the matter and work through whatever was there. I sincerely meant it. I mean, after all, how do you simply throw away 17 ½ years of marriage and all of our history together? Sadly, to my disappointment, there was never a reply.

In February, we celebrated my youngest daughter's 12th birthday at a bowling alley. Several of my family members came to try and make it fun and memorable for her. My husband drove down from Green Bay also. Needless to say, there were awkward moments but, thankfully, no *Jerry Springer* episodes! The next day he headed back to Green Bay, or so I thought. Later, I found out through a friend in Madagascar, that he had driven to Chicago after the birthday party and then flew to Madagascar to sell off all that we had left there, unbeknownst to me.

A few weeks after the birthday party, my oldest daughter asked me a question, "How can you work on the marriage when you are here and Dad is in Green Bay?" I remember that moment very clearly. God used that question to pierce my heart with His truth and to alter the course of the three of us. She was right. I didn't want to hear it, let alone admit it, but she was right. The more I pondered her question and the possibility of moving the girls and me to Green Bay, the more I realized there would be significant ramifications for all of us, but especially for me. I understood that if I took the girls to Green Bay, no matter what happened, reconciliation or not, we would most likely end up staying there until both girls graduated from high school, which was a minimum of 6 years. Even though I hated to admit it, I knew it would be the best thing for the girls. They were struggling to adjust where we were, since everything was new and unexpected. I knew that in Green Bay they were at least already familiar with the area and had friends they had made in the school there too. But most importantly, I realized it would give them the best chance of maintaining a relationship with their father. He had been a very good father to the girls up to this point, and, even though I hated to acknowledge this truth, I knew it would be the healthiest thing for them to be able to continue having him in close proximity and involved in their lives.

On the other hand, I grew up in Ohio and this was the first time I had lived back here since I went to college. I had family just a few short hours away. They had provided much needed love and support to the girls and me during this time. Besides that, my home church was only about a half an hour away from where we were staying now. I also had some very dear friends, and longtime mentors in my life, which lived less than an hour drive away. Since we had been here they'd lent me a car to use, while other friends helped me find a reasonably priced, mechanically sound car to purchase. Leaving here meant leaving the only real support system and security I had. I knew if I wanted to, I could get a job and find a place for the three of us to settle down and live near family. The girls would have a chance to get to know and see my side of the family more than they had ever had the opportunity to do so before.

To make matters worse, I didn't want my husband to 'win.' I was angry with him and wanted him to pay!! I wanted to hurt him like he had hurt the girls and me. It seemed to me that he had gotten his way up to this point and it didn't seem right or fair to me since he was the one who screwed up! He was the one who didn't want to do this and wasn't even trying to work things out. He was the one who walked away from us. Now we have to be the ones to follow him? "God, this isn't fair!" I screamed to Him in my mind. The battle was very real and I realized that whatever choice I made would hold lasting consequences for both the girls and me. When I boiled it all down, I had to admit to myself that there was really only one battle. Would I obey what the Spirit was saying to me through my daughter or not?

I prayed about this for several days. Honestly, it was more like an internal wrestling match. It seemed so unfair to me that God would even ask this. Why should I give up my family and my support system to go and work on a marriage that my husband had walked away from and didn't seem at all interested in trying to repair? If I go to Green Bay, won't I be going into his territory? His family? His home church, etc.?

In all honesty, I knew there were some people who truly loved me there too. We had based out of Green Bay for a year and a half in 1999 during my medical rehabilitation after an accident we had on the mission field in December of 1998. During that time, I had made some very dear friends in that area. However, I countered in my mind, it was not the same as my family and my home church in the best of circumstances. And, needless to say, these were not the best of circumstances.

Finally, emotionally exhausted from the fight, I surrendered to Jesus and His will. And for those brief moments, when I allowed myself to put anger and emotions aside, I knew deep down in my heart I wanted a reconciled marriage and family above my own will or anything else, even if it came at a very high price. I chose to fast for 3 days and invited some of my prayer partners to join with me, if they felt God leading them to do so. I was asking God to give me the battle plan for the spiritual warfare we were in, the strength that was needed for the fight and to give me a broken heart for my husband; a love that can only come from Him, since I knew that my natural love was not sufficient. I was also asking God to give the girls special grace for another transition which would help them quickly settle back into Green Bay.

So, on March 11th, five days prior to my oldest daughter's 14th birthday, we arrived back in Green Bay with our 6 suitcases in tow. Three days later the girls were registered and back in school. God, being the faithful Father that He is, provided for the three of us yet again. Through the generosity of a friend's parents, a fully furnished house was made available for us to live in until I could secure employment and a permanent place for us to live. My only responsibility was to pay for the utilities. Over and over I found myself amazed with God's faithfulness and the continued kindness and generosity of His people. However, I still wrestled with a lot of anger - the whole mess I found myself in, another transition, needing to find a job - these were just a few of the reasons I struggled.

The girls also were anxious about starting over again. Especially since it had been only 7 short months since we said goodbye to everyone here. I wondered how difficult it would be for them to explain to all of their friends why they were back and wished I could do something about it. I had to trust God to somehow use this entire season to help them grow into stronger, more compassionate women.

My oldest daughter celebrated her 14th birthday with cosmic bowling, a movie and 3 girls spending the night. I know she would have preferred a party with more friends but I just couldn't pull it together. And, because we were staying in someone's furnished home, I was more concerned about the possibility of something getting broken. Her dad came over for dinner and cosmic bowling, to help celebrate, spending about 2 hours with us. It was very hard for me as he continued to blame everything on me. That not only baffled me but made me angry! I prayed and asked God to help me not get riled by his words and attitude, rather to be thankful for the beautiful daughter we were celebrating.

These same people, who graciously provided our lodging, offered me a part-time job cleaning at their Community Based Residential

Facility (CBRF) to help make ends meet until I could find full-time work. Over the course of a few months, I found another part-time position at another CBRF, did respite for CBRF owners and landed an on-call position at a local hospital as chaplain. Somehow this hodge-podge of jobs, a good amount of thrifty living and financial blessings from Jesus sprinkled in here and there, provided what was needed to make ends meet for the girls and me.

I continued to reach out to my husband, asking when we could start counseling together or take some steps toward working on our marriage. Sadly, there was always an excuse. After some time, and many requests, I finally asked, "You really don't want to work on our marriage, do you?" His response was something along the lines of, "Maybe you guessed it right."

So here we were again. He was refusing to go to counseling here too. It all seemed so unreal. What really happened to us? Where was it our marriage began to drift and how could I have avoided this shipwreck? How can he simply walk away from our 17 ½ -year marriage, our family and our history together? These recurring questions seemed to swirl around my mind without ever finding an answer. Welcomed or not, anger, shame and bitterness were friends that remained close by, always ready to come and join me at a moment's notice. How could this be our reality? We were missionaries, who loved God, loved each other…what happened? I came here hoping that this might make a difference. Now, I'm really stuck here in Green Bay. His territory, his playground. *God…this isn't fair*!!! Once again, my three familiar friends, anger, shame and bitterness accompanied me. This time I allowed them to gain an even tighter grip.

On Wednesday, May 2nd, my husband phoned to tell me that we had been called to a meeting with our credentialing district on Monday, the 7th. I hoped this meeting might serve to start the process of healing and working toward salvaging our marriage. A few days later we went. It proved to be a challenging meeting. The district officials were compassionate, yet firm and honest. I felt that God was moving, if only in the supernatural arena. As of yet, there was not too much that could be seen in the natural realm. Finally, there was at least a nugget of truth! My husband admitted to having an emotional affair, yet continued to deny any and all allegations of a sexual one. I wrestled within, trying to figure out what the truth actually was. I wondered if I had overreacted and misjudged him. On the other hand, I knew in my gut that he must have been unfaithful sexually - there were too many signs. Yet up to this point I had no actual proof, just a lot of allegations from different sources that all seemed to point that way. Once again, I began to pray and ask God to bring the truth to light since I had decided several months back not to waste my time or emotional energy playing detective. I reminded myself that God is faithful and can be trusted to bring what I need when I need it.

My husband's credentials as a minister with our denomination were suspended at that meeting. They offered the possibility of reinstatement upon successful completion of the rehabilitation process, a minimum of one year. This included weekly counseling, a monthly meeting with a local pastor, attending a local church of our denomination and meeting with the district officials quarterly. To my surprise, he actually agreed to go through with it, for which I was truly excited and grateful! This was my first real glimmer of hope.

In spite of the progress this seemed to offer, I felt in desperate need of prayer. I had some friends who became regular prayer partners during this whole saga and I emailed them somewhat regularly with prayer requests. On this update, I shared with them that I was struggling with depression and felt like quitting. I asked them to pray for me specifically that the enemy would not gain a stronghold in my heart or mind. I knew the enemy was fighting hard and that this was, and would continue to be, a spiritual battle. I was truly grateful for these faithful family members and friends who were standing with me in this battle through prayer.

In spite of the confusion, frustration and pain, God continued to show Himself faithful to me. A few months back I had begun to think about purchasing a home in order to run an adult foster care of my own. I started looking for a place that would give the girls and me a sense of permanency and provide me the ability to earn a steady income while at the same time giving the flexibility to be mom as the girls needed.

About 7 weeks had passed since our meeting with the district officials, and up to this point, my husband had not followed through with any of the requirements. Any hope I had of us working on our marriage and moving back together were greatly diminishing. I knew I had to find a permanent place for the girls and me to call home. I spoke with him about it. He was not happy about that and told me that if I continued to try and control things by purchasing a home then he would not pursue reconciliation since I was not being submissive. Well, I thought to myself, you haven't pursued reconciliation to this point, so we are no worse for the wear.

It wasn't long and God directed me to the perfect fixer-upper that would soon become our home; structurally sound but needing a good amount of TLC and elbow grease. A few weeks later, on June 30th, I sent my husband two letters. The first explained why I was choosing to purchase a house. I went on to tell him that this had nothing to do with control, but rather giving the three of us a place where we could settle in, put up pictures and have a permanent place for us to call home. I continued by saying it would also provide income for the girls and me in proceeding to do adult foster care. The second letter was legal, releasing him of any liability from the future purchase of my home. Thankfully, he signed the paper and I was able to move forward with purchasing a place for the three of us to call home!

I still remember working on obtaining the mortgage and receiving the call when I'd been approved. "Jesus," I said nervously, sending a prayer of half desperation and anticipation, "please close the door if You're not in this 'cuz I'm in deep, deep trouble if I'm doing this on my own and it isn't You!" But the gracious hand of the Lord was with me and He was in it, proving it over and over again by His miraculous provision over the first 6 months I owned it.

To this very day, I continue to stand amazed at how God did this! In reality, I shouldn't have gotten that loan. The fact was, when all the numbers were crunched, without Jesus and His supernatural help, I didn't have the ability to make the payments. But God brought the right person at the right time to help me complete the paperwork I needed to prove my ability to pay. He gave me the right mortgage broker, references, the right letters from our mission board, etc., and possibly even a blind eye to the loan officer at the bank. To my amazement, I eventually received the call that I was approved for the loan. Scared, but excited, I knew a new season was on its way!

We moved into our new home by mid-August, after taking a few weeks to clean, paint, remove and replace things. It wasn't long until this house had become our home. I was amazed at how God had taken our 6 suitcases and a very limited budget, and filled it with everything we needed. I was grateful for garage sales and St. Vincent de Paul's Thrift Store. Our decor and furniture certainly wasn't anything fancy, but it matched, it was ours, and it was home! We even had a *Thanks for Your Help* party, inviting all those who joined in the painting, moving furniture, etc. to celebrate with us. Afterwards, we took time to pray over the home and dedicate it to the Lord. Looking back, I remain amazed at God's supernatural provision - how He managed to sprinkle small financial miracles while stretching my meager earnings in order to make the monthly mortgage. I couldn't thank God enough for His faithfulness to the girls and me. He truly had been my husband and provider during this time.

Not only had this year brought personal crisis to our family, but sadly the ripples of impact were also felt within our home church, where the girls and I were attending. It seemed many of the church people were at a loss as well, as to how to interact with us. Many were struggling with their own sense of grief or disappointment regarding our situation and did not know what to say or do with their fallen missionary family. There were some who would literally avoid walking near me so they wouldn't have to talk to me. It was awkward, and it stung too. It wasn't that they didn't care. I know they cared. Nor was it that they wanted to be hurtful. The truth was that most of them had supported our work as missionaries for years and they were hurting too.

Many of them had known my husband since he came to Christ as a teenager and began attending church here. They had prayed for us as a family and regularly supported us financially. They had even given sacrificially to buy a truck for our evangelism efforts in Madagascar and were heartbroken, crying and interceding for our family when we were involved in a serious accident with that same vehicle only a few years prior to all of this. They had offered moral support as we based out of this church during our 18-month medical furlough after the accident, while I went through rehab learning to walk again. They cheered me on as I went from wheelchair to walker to independently walking again. The truth was that this church had invested in us and clearly loved us. They had even sent us off with a BIG farewell, complete with renting a limo to take us to the airport when we returned to Africa less than a year ago.

Now, unexpectedly, we were back. Only this time it wasn't a medical issue. That would have been more palatable. After all, what do you say to a missionary couple that has a fractured marriage, is separated, and showing no signs of reconciliation? We had let them down and I felt every bit of the weight of it. They didn't know what to say or do to make things right again. Neither did I. We attended there for several more months. However, after I'd talked to the pastor about it, we eventually transferred to another church, one that had also supported us but who hadn't known us quite as personally.

In the Midwest, fall is a beautiful time of year. However, since I'd been in missions and enjoyed living in warm weather climates, there was always a small part of me that mourned the passing of summer with the onset of fall. I knew that winter, with all of its snow and cold, was just around the corner. This year seemed to carry with it an even deeper, more profound cold. A chill in my very being that, at times, couldn't seem to be shaken. And with that came a certain sadness. You see, in our denomination, fall is the time that missions is emphasized the most. Normally this would be accompanied by excitement and preparation for a heavy speaking schedule and travel, as opportunities to minister at churches usually abounded. This year was quite different, containing no speaking engagements or travel. To make matters worse, the church where we were now making our home was gearing up for its annual emphasis on missions.

Since our return, whenever anyone spoke on or emphasized missions, there was always something from within that wanted to come alive and yet seemed to wither all at the same time. That old familiar enemy of my soul didn't miss an opportunity. He was there throwing shame and feelings of failure, reminding me of each and every person who had been let down by our return home. And, sadly, I allowed some of that to pierce my heart. Any emphasis on missions also served as a reminder that my call had, at least for this season, been ripped from me, leaving a gaping hole. Departing so quickly from the land of our calling only added to the loss, not allowing us adequate time for proper good-byes or closure. This sometimes seemed extremely hard to endure. No, this fall I was not looking forward to a series of special meetings that focused on the need to go. My heart still felt too tender, too vulnerable.

During this year's mission emphasis, tears came quickly and flowed freely at the altar as I poured my heart out to God. The hit on my family, the displacement from Madagascar, and the pain I saw in my girls from time to time was almost too much to bear. All of this disappointment came from deep within, spilling onto my cheeks through tears, forming heartfelt prayers back up to my heavenly Father from my innermost being. Oddly enough, as the enemy of my soul barraged me with all of the negative ramifications, I brought them to God in the form of tears and, often, wordless prayers. And in God's infinite goodness, He graciously brought bits of healing and cleansing with each act of surrender of anger, bitterness, disappointment, shame and grief.

And, even though it seemed I didn't hear Him like I used to, I knew He was faithful and doing a work I couldn't see. He had proven that time and time again. And He was proving it to me again with each and every tear that was shed, as He gently cleansed and restored another part of my soul.

By the beginning of January 2002, I had the first resident in my home for the adult foster care. January brought with it other changes as well. The girls had been with me, for the most part, full-time during our first year of separation, staying at their father's place only intermittently. He had stated in mid-November that he wanted to have joint custody of the girls, but had not done much to follow up on that. And I was certainly not going to encourage it. Even though there was still the financial strain of feeding, housing and clothing three females, and dealing with all of our emotional ups and downs by myself, I loved being the girls' mom and was doing my very best to establish family in this new paradigm. Nonetheless, with the turn of the year, my husband had set up a few appointments with a pro-se divorce litigation service, which is basically a do-it-yourself divorce when nothing is contested; agreeing on everything from child custody, to division of property and debts, etc. He was beginning to follow through on joint custody.

In regard to the girls and joint custody, my initial reaction was to go for the jugular and fight him with everything that was in me. After all, I thought, Isn't it his fault we are all in this mess? Why did he wait until now, a year after our separation, to decide he wanted them in his life more? My emotions were raw. I was angry that, up until this point, he had made no real effort to make the girls a priority. Nor did he try to work on our marriage, despite repeated attempts on my end to let him know I was willing to go to counseling and do whatever it took to make things work. It made perfect sense to me - if he didn't want to rebuild our marriage and family as we knew it, then why should I cooperate with him to get more time with the girls? I wanted to punish him…make him pay. And yet, on the other hand, I had seen the pain that the lack of relationship with their father had caused the girls up to this point.

OBEDIENCE: IS IT WORTH IT?

In my mind, I argued with God. In my flesh, I wanted to pit the girls against their father. I knew that was totally within my power and I could easily do it. At this point, I didn't trust their dad or his motives. My girls' emotions were raw too. They'd been hurt and disappointed as well. I didn't want them to be hurt any more than they had already experienced. I continued to wrestle with this in prayer. In the end, I knew what was best for the girls and I didn't like it. Having an increased, consistent relationship with their father was what was best for them in the long run. Once again, I breathed a prayer, "God, you have to help me with this. I can't do it in my own strength and I really don't even want to."

So, it began, joint custody. I had always hated the thought of the girls having to change households and for me to have to share them in this way. Initially, I would cry every time I dropped them off to go to their father's house or after he came to pick them up. I never wanted this for my daughters or me. I never wanted my family to look like this. Nevertheless, after a few months, we seemed to establish a rhythm and routine. Eventually, this new groove of back and forth had become our new reality, like it or not. And I never did.

In terms of my relationship with their father, for the most part, it had been in limbo. No real communication. No real opportunities to even try to repair what was damaged. He had mentioned divorce several times, and was pushing for us to go the pro se route. Besides the fact that I no longer trusted him to equitably divide our assets, the biggest issue was that I didn't agree to the divorce!! I truly wanted reconciliation and believed in God's ability to redeem our marriage and family. I didn't want to throw away our now 18-year history and permanently fragment our family. Yet, it seemed as if the gulf between us was widening and, no matter what I did, I felt powerless to do anything about it.

I continued to pray and, with every possible opportunity, to make my desire of reconciliation known. I truly desired for us to figure out exactly what was broken, where we went wrong, and how we could work toward reconciling our marriage and family. I expressed this to him in various ways, such as sending a card, a letter or email. And, whenever possible, in person. Even though there were many dynamics at play and it looked very improbable, if not impossible, I still knew God was able and could redeem our family, if we gave Him the opportunity. After all, He is the God of all hope and the impossible and He had proven His faithfulness to the girls and me over and over again.

To my surprise, my husband had landed a staff position at an independent church. I had no idea what he told the hiring pastor, but if it was the truth it would be highly unlikely that my husband would have been able to land this position. My girls were surprised and confused by this too and they asked me about it. After we talked it through, we decided that we needed to leave this in the hands of the Lord and continue to pray for their father.

As time marched by, I managed, by God's grace, to keep myself positioned for reconciliation; keeping my heart tender toward God and my husband, yet continuing to move forward in life. Conversely, I did not want reconciliation at any cost. Behavioral changes had to be made. It is impossible to rebuild a relationship if there is not true repentance. Real repentance produces changed behavior, resulting in the ability to work toward rebuilding trust. In the midst of it all, I did my best to provide as stable an environment as possible for the girls when they were with me and, for the most part, to remain positive in my attitude. Except for the movement of the kids back and forth, nothing else seemed to change in terms of progress towards reconciliation.

OBEDIENCE: IS IT WORTH IT?

# Chapter Four

—✦—

# THE UNEXPECTED

*"There is always a lesson of a lifetime to learn in every betrayal."*
*Edmond Mbiaka*

SOMETIME IN FEBRUARY of 2002, after having received only one child support payment, my husband asked if I would consider dropping it. He bargained that if I did that, then he would consider counseling. I considered this a no brainer and dropped it, since I was more interested in saving our marriage and family than the financial aspect of it all.

March brought a few big changes. First, my husband was dismissed from our denomination as a minister for not following through with the rehabilitation process. And second, it presented the first real indication of the reality of divorce. He had, to my amazement, followed through with making a counseling appointment and invited me to come. I wholeheartedly accepted. I was apprehensive, but hopeful that this could be a positive sign and possibly a turning point. That glimmer of hope soon came to a screeching halt. Within five minutes of the start of our appointment, he stated, in no uncertain terms, that he wanted a divorce. I felt totally blind-sided, along with countless other emotions. Hurt, anger, and sadness seemed to come from within with a vengeance. Thoughts swirled around in my mind. How could I have been so dumb? Let him have the stupid divorce! What does it matter anyway? At least this limbo would finally be over! After silencing the questions in my mind, I somehow managed to find my voice and my resolve. Once again, I calmly declined, stating that I would not cooperate with a pro se divorce and wanted to spend my energy working toward saving our marriage rather than on how to divorce. He abruptly left the room.

For a few moments, the counselor and I sat in stunned silence, both trying to regroup from what just happened. Finally, the counselor stated, "I'm sorry. I didn't know this was going to be an ambush." "Neither did I," I replied, as I stood up, gathered my things and left.

After I had time to collect my thoughts, I knew deep down what God still wanted, an opportunity to be given to Him to show Himself powerful to make beauty from ashes. To perform a miracle, not a divorce, something only He could do. Would He ever get that chance? I wondered. I honestly didn't know. That decision wasn't totally in my hands. When I wasn't angry or hurt, I wanted what God wanted too. I would obey. Once again, I would wait. I would choose to stay in limbo and stick to what I knew to be God's will and my own, reconciliation. Once again, I uttered a prayer that had become commonplace to me, "God, I need you to help me continue to trust you. I need you to give me the grace to remain waiting. I desperately need you to give me the faith to trust you and believe that all things are possible with You. And to know that no matter what happens, You have my life, and that of my girls, in Your hands."

My resolve only increased to do nothing in terms of filing any paperwork for a divorce and to steadfastly trust God with the outcome. I persisted in prayer. I continued to ask God to work in my heart and do what He needed to do in me to make me the wife my husband needed me to be.

Once again, he brought up doing a pro se divorce. I felt uncomfortable with it on multiple levels. I restated that I wasn't going to do any paperwork in regard to filing for a divorce. After some discussion, I finally replied, "If you want a divorce so bad you will have to file for it." It wasn't but a few weeks later that I was served divorce papers.

It's funny what your mind does when placed in a strange situation. I remember thinking, so it really does happen like I've seen a time or two in the movies. Someone knocks on the door, tells you you're being served and hands you something to sign to verify you are receiving the paperwork. I took the envelope in one hand, signed the paper verifying that I had received it with the other hand, and slowly walked back through the door into my house. I sat down on my couch, unhurriedly opened the envelope and began to peruse the contents that I knew undoubtedly lie within.

To be truthful, I honestly don't remember much more about that day, except the above scenario. I'm sure I mulled it all over in my mind, letting the reality of what had just happened sink in and began to process what this meant for me. After a few days, I began to seek out godly counsel from those I trusted as to what I should do. I did have one pastor tell me that I should not 'take a brother to court' and acquiesce to the pro se. The reality was, I wasn't taking him to court, he was taking me. A true brother, as I saw it, would be wanting the same thing I did, to obey God and do everything in our power to try and rebuild our relationship, not permanently tear it apart. Another glaring issue in this whole scenario is that in order for a pro se divorce to work, there has to be trust between the two parties involved, ensuring that everything is done in the best interest of everyone. When one's only pursuit is that which goes against God's Word, I considered it unwise to do something legally in a relationship where trust had long been broken and nothing had been done or even attempted to restore it.

It had been about three months now that my husband had been on staff at a local independent church. He asked me to set up a meeting with the senior pastor as he wanted to talk with us. Finally! I thought to myself. I was more than ready for this meeting, as I felt it should have taken place before he was ever hired. It was only a matter of days before the three of us sat together in the senior pastor's office. He began to talk to the two of us, mandating that we get back together and proceeded to set a timeline of about 6 weeks for us to begin living together again. I was totally surprised by his edict since it was the first time I was meeting this pastor. I responded by telling him that he could not mandate anything, but I was, however, willing to work toward reconciliation on the following conditions: That my husband demonstrates a commitment to our marriage above anything else (ministry, career, etc.), a sincere, repentant heart acknowledging any wrong behavior, some kind of rehab program or counseling for both of us to work toward fully re-establishing our marriage, and finally, and most importantly, *no other women.*

I continued to tell the pastor that my husband may have fooled him, but he was not fooling me and that he was seeing another woman. I continued to state that *if* there was true repentance and changed behavior we could begin to talk about things like reconciliation. However, I was not going to reconcile with someone who pursued divorce more than he did reconciliation and who continued to see other women. Once again, allegations were denied. I concluded by stating *if* there was true repentance and changed behavior then I was more than willing to talk about working toward reconciliation. Needless to say, that meeting did not end well and I left feeling angry and frustrated with the entire situation.

I was getting very tired of this game, but at least this time I had more of a leg to stand on in regard to my suspicions. Friends of mine had seen my husband on his motorcycle with a woman with dark hair riding with him on the bike, verifying what I had suspected. My girls had unknowingly confirmed some of the same with comments they had made to me as well.

It became more and more clear to me that *true reconciliation* can only take place when both parties are willing and there is a sincere

OBEDIENCE: IS IT WORTH IT?

*repentant heart* which is demonstrated by *changed behavior.* "God," I prayed, "that is what I desire. I don't know what to do. Please help us!"

It was about six weeks after that meeting, on a Sunday night, that I was sitting upstairs in one of my daughter's bedroom. The girls were with their father and my residents were downstairs so I took advantage of the opportunity to be alone with God. Since this whole thing began I had been asking God to bring truth to light and show me what was happening. It was so frustrating to hear allegations and the subsequent denials that always seemed to accompany them. To my surprise, I heard a knock on my daughter's bedroom door, which pulled me from my own thoughts and brought me back to reality. Hmmm, who could that be? I wondered. My residents never came up to my daughters' rooms. I got up off the bed and opened the door. To my surprise, there was a dark-haired woman whom I did not know standing there.

Almost instantly I knew in my spirit that she was having an affair with my husband. She politely apologized for interrupting me and quickly told me that one of my residents had let her in and told her I was upstairs. I invited her into the bedroom, signaled for her to sit down beside me and asked what I could do for her. "You're not going to like me very well," she said as she quickly diverted her eyes from looking into mine to looking at the floor, and proceeded to tell me that she was having an affair with my husband. She continued to say that my husband had told her I was unwilling to reconcile and she believed him. She had somehow found out, however, that was not true and that I was, in reality, pursuing reconciliation. She asked me to forgive her and stated that she was going to break it off with him. I asked her point blank if they had been sexually active (since I knew it would later be denied). She ashamedly lowered her eyes and nodded that they had. I thanked her for having the courage to come and talk honestly with me. I also told her I forgave her and then prayed for her. After the prayer, we talked for a few more minutes. Then I asked if she would be willing to do something for me. After making my case, and not a little persuasion, she reluctantly agreed.

I called my husband and told him I needed to speak with him right away, something had come up. He grudgingly agreed and said he would be over in a few minutes. Meanwhile, I hid the woman in my other daughter's bedroom, situated kitty-corner in the hall. I left the door open so, once he arrived, she could hear our conversation in the other bedroom. He arrived and came up to the bedroom where it appeared we could talk privately. I told him I had heard from someone that he was having affair with _____ and I wanted to ask him face-to-face if it was true. He immediately denied it and began to explain that she had come on to him but he told her to leave him alone because he was married. Like a scene from a movie, within seconds, the woman who had been hiding came flying out of the other bedroom and confronted him face-to-face. In no uncertain terms, she angrily confronted him on his lies. Their quarreling back and forth went on for several minutes. It was as if I was watching a scene from a movie or soap opera. My husband eventually stormed out of the house, continuing to deny that they were having an affair. I thanked her again for her courage and for coming to ask my forgiveness, and also for being willing to stay and allow me to confront him with the situation, knowing it would cause her to confront him, too. At least now I had some proof. The poor woman left, angry, hurt, and amazed that the entire scenario had been blamed on her and denied by my husband. At that moment, I honestly felt sorry for her.

Sitting for a few moments somewhat stunned by this evening's turn of events, I replayed it all in my mind. Did this really just happen? I asked myself, somewhat amused at the situation and how surreal it all seemed. I thanked God for bringing this courageous woman to my home and for confirming what I had known in my heart for a long time, but had never being able to verify. This certainly brought an interesting conclusion to my prayer time!

My husband resigned from the church a few days later.

It was becoming more and more evident, barring a miracle, that the divorce was going to happen. My husband continued to make no effort to acknowledge or change his behavior. After spending time in prayer, and talking with others who had traversed the ugly road of divorce, I did not feel that it would be in my best interest or that of my daughters to continue on my own without a lawyer. I made appointments and interviewed a couple of lawyers, trying to determine whom I felt would be the best fit to represent me. I had no idea how I was going to pay for a lawyer and began to pray about that too. With the average cost of an attorney being $150-$300 an hour, I was thankful that at least the initial consultation was free. I knew divorce would be expensive. When discussing this and praying about it with a long-time prayer partner and dear friend of mine, she and her husband graciously offered to lend me the money, interest free. I could not have been more grateful for their offer and knew that God was going before me...even in this unwanted legal battle.

In the midst of all of this I had a very long talk with my girls. I told them more fully what had been happening. Although I left out a lot of details, I told them enough to be able to understand why I was not going to try and fight the divorce any longer. They both stated that they had already known it in their hearts but hadn't wanted to admit it to themselves. I told them I could certainly understand how hard it was for them to have to grapple with this. I also let them know that if the divorce did go through I would look forward and not back. In other words, I would not be looking for their father in the rear-view mirror and would begin to view myself as a single parent. I continued by saying *IF* God brought us back together that would be His problem and not mine. I was still open to whatever God wanted but did not have the emotional energy to keep this up as the reality of reconciliation continued to diminish with each passing day that the court date got closer. We prayed and committed their father, our family and the future to the Lord.

By the end of September, I settled on a lawyer. I remember telling him that I was not going for the jugular, but wanted what was right and fair for my daughters and me. After all, even in this unwelcome divorce, I wanted to try to respond in a way that would somehow please my heavenly Father. It's funny, even during this unsolicited and unwanted season in my life when it seemed that my prayers were hitting the ceiling and falling right back down on my head and hearing God's voice for direction appeared, at times, impossible, I was amazed that, more often than not, I continued to see His provision and faithfulness. And on rare occasions, I felt a closeness with God in ways I had never before experienced.

I had determined, going through this, that I would do my best to continue to do what I knew to be right: continue to read my Bible, continue to voice my prayers to Him, continue to try to listen for His voice and continue to remain faithful to my church. I also surrounded myself with trustworthy, godly friends who would give godly counsel and speak truth to me, even when I didn't want to hear it. I was truly grateful for those few, but close friends that I had allowed into my darkest hour, seeing my most vulnerable self. They walked beside me as confidants, counselors and advisors. Their voices were invaluable to me in this season, often offering what I could not see by myself. At times, they consoled me. Other times they exhorted me, rebuked me or challenged me to continue to do what I knew to be right, which most of the time seemed to be the more difficult path, but also the best one.

There were calls and letters from the lawyer with occasional court appearances. Each one of them had a price tag attached to it. Not just financially, but emotionally as well. I remember thinking that this process seemed to drag on and on. Maybe it had been because of the added first year of us being back in the States and the seeming limbo. Now, here I was, more than a year and a half back in the States with no resolution in my marriage, attorney fees and not even a divorce to show for it. Sigh. It seemed as if I was in a holding pattern or sitting on the back burner of a stove, neither of which I liked very much.

The kids continued with their back and forth routine. My heart ached for them. I knew this was not how God intended children to live. Try as I might to avoid it, it seemed my girls occasionally ended up in the middle of some issue between my husband and me. Oh, how I hated divorce!! Now I realized even more deeply why God hates it too. I had understood it, having grown up in this environment as a child with divorced parents, a half-brother, stepparents and stepbrothers and sisters. It certainly was no picnic. As an adult that made me never want it for my family even more. Yet, despite my best efforts, here it was, pommeling the front door of my life, rattling the framework of my family like an unwelcome tornado. If our current path continued, I knew our lives would be permanently rearranged in the not too distant future. In the midst of it all, I reminded myself that we would survive, somehow by the grace of God, but I wasn't exactly sure how much damage the girls and I would sustain in the process.

I remember choosing not to live in a state of gloom and despair; rather, I allowed God to continue to keep me moving forward in Him. In life. In spite of. Yes, I was still married to a person who was going, for all practical purposes, in the opposite direction of my life in almost everything. Despite that, I could still *choose* to make progress in my own life and emotionality. And by God's grace, I did.

One thing God taught me through this process, as I described it to others, was to unhook myself from my husband's roller coaster. In other words, I was often aware that he was going up, down or around a corner at breakneck speed, but I didn't have to ride it with him. I could choose to emotionally detach, to a healthy degree, and live my life in surrender to Jesus, trading my crazy for the fruit of the Spirit: love, joy, peace, patience, goodness, kindness, gentleness, faithfulness and self-control. Once I began to realize that, even though we were still married and most of his choices were not ones I would have made, I could watch from a distance, pray and seek God's wisdom for every situation and trust Him to cover me through it. I learned that I didn't have to ride every emotion that came my way, whether my husband's or mine. I could choose to stay off the proverbial roller coaster by staying an emotionally healthy distance from it all and allowing God to provide stability in my life and that of my daughters, in spite of the circumstances. This was a valuable lesson for me. I still use that technique today in other situations.

Instead of allowing myself to wallow in sorrow or self-pity when the girls weren't with me, I began to make the most of my time. I got involved in things on my off weeks. I led a small group in my home. I volunteered more at church. I picked up extra on-call hours at work. I had coffee dates with girlfriends. And when the girls were with me, I cleared my schedule as much as I possibly could to give us more quality time together. I was truly amazed at how God redeemed the time I had with my daughters. I even got to the point where I could occasionally joke about how some people might find it a blessing to send their teen-agers off for a week. Even though I hated this unexpected, unwelcome division of time with my girls, I was amazed to see how, even in this, God was producing fruit in all three of our lives because of it.

Don't misunderstand me. Things were not perfect. Neither was I. One scene comes to my memory quite vividly, and I think it always will. As one daughter looked on, the other daughter began to blame everything bad in her life on our divorce. Her words hit me particularly hard that day. I gave her more than an earful as I retorted with a litany of how I hadn't wanted this to happen, how I hated dividing my time with them and seeing them come and go and how it had impacted me as well, among other things. I'm quite sure I ranted and raved for a solid 20 minutes or so with hardly taking a breath!! Then I proceeded to remind her that she had choices to make on how she would process this in her life. "There will always be someone to lick your wounds, to sympathize with you and tell you what a rough life you have had and there is some truth to that." I continued by reminding her that if she chose that route, sadly, she would stay wounded and never move beyond all of this. However, if she chose to admit this sucks and would learn to grow through it, she could become a stronger woman and even help others down the road because of it. I'm thankful both of my daughters chose to heed that advice. Needless to say, neither of my daughters ever chose to use that argument again! I think we all learned through that experience and grew a little bit more that day.

OBEDIENCE: IS IT WORTH IT?

I could tell you several stories of my less than best behavior. Sadly, I had my share of them. But I can also tell you, by the grace of God and my willful decision to obey Him, I had more of the ones where I decided to allow Jesus to shine, even when everything in me wanted to retaliate or speak a bitter word. I chose to apply my life verse, "Whatever happens, conduct yourself in a manner worthy of the Gospel of Christ." (Philippians 1:27a) That verse has helped me walk through many a situation in my life, not simply my divorce.

Every one of us, like my daughter, is given choices as we walk through circumstances in life. Divorce was no exception. How will I react to false accusations or harsh words? Would I do my best to reflect Jesus or will I let it rip just once to make myself feel good? In reality, we usually feel good for the moment, but that single instance has the potential to leave lasting, devastating consequences.

When tempted to spout off or retaliate, I did my best to remind myself that in the end I wanted reconciliation. What if we both allowed God to perform the miracle of reconciliation? Would I regret anything I had said to my girls? To my friends and family? Was I, by my words, working toward a foundation of the possibility of reconciliation or was I tearing that foundation apart? These simple thoughts helped guard my tongue from more than one flippant response, and for that, I am truly grateful to God for His grace.

The girls and I had our share of tears and challenges as well. But I also worked very hard at rebuilding what was clearly becoming our newly defined family, at least for now. I remember the time I took the girls to get our first family picture after the separation. I'm not sure about them, but for me it was a defining moment. I decided that no matter what happened in our marriage, we (the girls and I) were going to survive as family. And, by God's grace, not just survive, but thrive. I knew it was possible, so I set my resolve to do everything in my power to make that possibility become a reality.

By this time finances were getting better; nonetheless, I still needed to budget wisely. However, when the pictures came in, I decided to spend the extra money on a picture ensemble that displayed these words: *Family: where hopes are shared and dreams are born.* It became a quasi-mission statement for me as we rebuilt our newly defined family. I displayed it proudly in our living room as a reminder to anyone who saw it that we *are* family, even though it was altered from what we knew before, and we would make it. That picture remains one of my favorites to this day. At the time, it symbolized hope for the three of us...no matter the outcome. Now, it serves as a reminder, a testimony of sorts, of God's incredible goodness and faithfulness during the most difficult season in our lives to this point.

Part of the divorce process required us to take a class called *The Successful Divorce.* While this isn't a bad idea, I remember thinking how paradoxical this was. If couples spent as much time trying to rebuild a broken marriage as they did at trying to have a successful divorce, might there just be more marriages saved in our country? What would happen if both parties were willing to wholeheartedly give God a chance to redeem a broken marriage? Oh, how I would love to see that!

Life continued to have its surprises. Because our mission board had been gracious to the girls and me, they extended our health insurance coverage beyond the normal allotted time. However, that grace period was coming to an end. Being proactive, I decided to schedule physicals and dental appointments for each of us since it was unclear when I would have coverage for our family again. In mid-September of 2002, as part of my annual physical, I had a routine mammogram. A day or two later their office called me back and asked me to come in to redo the mammogram. It wasn't long before I was sitting in an examining room waiting for a doctor to come in to give me the results. Many thoughts swirled through my mind. I tried to brush it off as routine, but as a hospital chaplain I had seen and heard a variety of medical scenarios and I knew that waiting for a doctor usually meant something abnormal had been found. I wondered what that would mean to me? I lifted a prayer to my heavenly Father. After all, He already knew the outcome, and I was confident that He who had walked with me so faithfully up to this point would see me through whatever was about to come.

I'm not sure how long I was lost in my thoughts when there was a knock on the door. An elderly doctor, with the comportment of a caring grandfather, reminding me of the TV doctor, Marcus Welby, walked into the room. He smiled warmly as his eyes met mine, bringing a calm into the situation. He introduced himself. I remember thanking God for him because he was so kind, gentle and reassuring. He asked me if anyone had come with me to this appointment. "No, I'm alone," I replied. At that moment, those words seemed to echo in the caverns of my soul. I truly felt alone. I could feel tears beginning to pool in my eyes as I waited for what was sure to be his pronouncement. He graciously took my hand and told me that the mammograms had most likely detected breast cancer. He said they couldn't be sure without further testing, but the mammograms had indicated it. He explained the need to do a biopsy.

Not knowing exactly what I was dealing with brought with it an accompanying uncertainty. I tried to keep things casual as I explained things to the girls. I kept them informed enough, but not so much that they had an extra burden to carry. The next few weeks were a blur; one appointment after another, the breast biopsy confirming cancer; lumpectomy and then treatment. I often describe that season like this: at one moment I was standing beside a train watching it go by; then, almost as if by some unforeseen force, I was sucked into it and was riding the train, travelling at a very fast speed, before I even had time to process what had happened.

The doctors had begun moving me toward the standard protocol treatment for this type and stage of cancer, which included radiation first and then was followed up by taking tamoxifen, a cancer drug. During the few weeks of preparation for this seemingly pre-determined route for my type of cancer, I walked through the maze of the measuring and marking for radiation, work, kids and a variety of other responsibilities. I also managed to make time to seek God and find out what treatment plan I felt was right for me. Based on all the facts I'd been given, medical prognosis and counsel I'd received, personal research done and conversations with trusted family and friends, I decided, in the end, to forego the traditional therapy, and chose alternative homeopathic treatment instead.

Once my decision was made there was mostly peace. Occasionally I would ask myself questions, such as: Did I make the right choice? What if this path isn't the right one? What would happen to my girls if...? It was at times like these that I had to trust God. I would remind myself that most likely I'd be fine, however, none of us are immortal. And even if I did die, I knew the One who would carry me to heaven would continue to carry my girls. Once more, my faith had an opportunity to grow in the midst of yet another storm.

There were times when life seemed overwhelming, and other times, when I truly seemed to be carried by God's grace. Sometimes I would recount the litany of things that had happened over the course of these past 21 months. And, depending on the day, I would remind myself of God's goodness to the girls and me, rehearsing how many ways He had been so faithful or I would cry out in despair, God, do you even remember my name? Of late, it seemed that my ability to hear God had greatly diminished since this whole thing began. I tried to remember the last time I'd clearly heard His gentle voice speaking to me. It had been a very long time. I wondered, was it simply the sheer exhaustion and numbness of trying to make it through each day of this very long season that had dulled my senses to the Spirit?

Interestingly, a few months prior to my cancer diagnosis, I had recommenced working on my Master's degree. Several months after the diagnosis, I was attending a class. It was one where you did pre-work ahead of time, attended several full days of classes, and then completed the course work afterwards by writing papers and taking a final exam. As I was leaving the final class to head to the airport to fly home, one of my fellow students, whom I had only met at this class, gave me a folded piece of paper and said he felt this was a message to me from the Lord. I thanked him, took the paper and slid it into my purse. I figured I would read it on my way to the airport. When I got settled into the van shuttling me and the other passengers from the hotel to the airport, I pulled out the paper. It simply read, *When the student is testing, the teacher is silent.* I smiled to myself and thought, Hmm. I must be missing something, 'cuz God, I was hoping for something more than this.

It's funny how in life some things need time in your spirit to germinate. A seed before it produces a sprig. A good idea before it becomes a reality. Such was the case with my note from God. I began to ponder the words that had been written on the paper, *When the student is testing, the teacher is silent.* I had never heard this saying before the moment I read it on the shuttle. As time passed, I reread it, and thought about it more. Finally the proverbial light bulb came on! God *seems* silent when we walk through tests. One thing I knew for sure, this was certainly a test in my life and God most certainly seemed silent! I sighed and mused, I just hope I pass. I know I longed for the day when things were normal again…whatever that might look like. And I truly longed to be out of the fog, hearing God's gentle voice on a more regular basis once again.

Days turned into weeks, weeks into months, and another fall was upon us. The annual missions emphasis at our church brought with it many tears. I reminded God, and myself, that I was ready to serve Him anywhere, even if that meant right here in Green Bay. I knew that, for now, I had been planted in the States, even if it was against my will. I determined to focus my energies on raising my two most important disciples, my daughters, and to bloom where I was planted, serving any way I could. It was a new kind of surrender that brought with it a greater measure of peace.

God had opened the door for me to serve as missions pastor at our church, which provided other ministry outlets for me. One of the highlights this year was that a team from our church was preparing to go to Nicaragua and build a school in January. I was able to celebrate the fact that others had caught the vision to go and minister cross-culturally. I longed for the day that God would reinstate my mission-ary call, but I reminded myself that now was not the time. Little did I know that God was up to something fun! Not long after that special emphasis on missions, the pastor pulled me aside and told me that someone had paid my way to go on that trip to Nicaragua! I couldn't believe it! I wondered how all of the details would fall into place for me to be able to go. I was confident, however, that if God provided the funds, He would clear the other logistical hurdles as well.

As things progressed through the court system it looked as though the divorce was not too far off. I had received a notice in that mail that we had a final court date of November 15, 2002. Honestly, I had mixed emotions. On one hand I thought, at least this part can be over and I can move on. On the other hand, it saddened my heart to think we had never really taken the opportunity to fight together for our marriage. One of the hardest things for me to swallow in all of this was that I never really felt like I understood what truly hap-pened. How did we get here in the first place? Why was my husband so unwilling to fight for our family and marriage? This pain, at times, seemed so unbearable. Was I flawed? Was everything my fault? What had I done that was so horrible that he would simply walk away from our 19 years of marriage? Our twenty-one years of history together? It seemed impossible to me to simply let go of that without at least an attempt to try to repair and rebuild it. Sigh. Just how many times have I wrestled with this in my mind?

A journal entry from 11-07-02:

"I look back on the last 2 years. It is hard to believe all that has transpired. I'm on the verge of a divorce. I only have my girls 50% of the time. I have breast cancer. Life often seems to be in fast forward and slow motion at the same time. While it has been painful, I have seen God's hand of provision, grace, strength. So many emotions. So many tears. I honestly never thought I could cry so much. This whole divorce issue is so much more than the cancer one. Or our accident for that matter. Not to diminish either, but they just are…the divorce is a betrayal of one who was loved deeply. One whom I believed in, trusted, declared to spend the rest of my life with. Broken dreams. Deception. Betrayal…" Well, it all appeared to be coming to an end shortly.

The week of November 15th was upon us. In light of our pending divorce becoming final, one of my sisters and sister-in-law had come to Green Bay to offer moral support. We enjoyed our time together. They were a breath of fresh air and a godsend. On Friday, the morning of the 15th, I was truly grateful I didn't have to face this day alone. We got the kids off to school and then about 8 am we began making our way to the courthouse for our appointed time of 8:30. Upon entering the courthouse, both my sister and sister-in-law remarked how beautiful the interior of the building was. It brought me back to the first time I had come into this building. Even though my heart was utterly broken, I was amazed at the beauty of this place. The atrium had a high vaulted ceiling, gold in color, with paintings set into it. Now that I had actually been here several times, more than I cared to, I had noticed some of the individual paintings. Despite the beauty of the place, there always seemed to be a coldness that resided here too. Was it possible that the coldness I sensed simply reflected the growing emptiness in the relationship between me and the man I still called my husband? In just a few brief moments that would no longer be a title that I would give to him.

There was one painting named *Justice*, which had a woman sitting as a judge. Below the painting was an inscription, which read, "There is no virtue so truly great and God like as justice." Justice, I mused. On more than one occasion I asked myself how such a beautiful place could serve for both good and evil? Didn't Scripture say, "What God has joined together let no man separate?" And today, with simply the hitting of a gavel and the stroke of a pen, my marriage would be terminated.

So, the three of us got settled into our seats and sat, with my lawyer, waiting. After a few minutes, my husband's lawyer showed up late...but not my husband. We three girls looked at each other wondering what was going on. I glanced at my lawyer. He had no clue as to why my husband had not shown up either. As a matter of fact, he never did show up. Our final hearing was now going to have to be rescheduled. I remember becoming very angry at this point. I asked my sister and sister-in-law in unbelief, "How could he start this whole thing, drag me through this, and not have the guts to show up for our final court date?" The fact that they had made arrangements to take off work and had come at their own expense to support me only served to fuel my anger! I told my lawyer that if I weren't a Christian I would have given in to a *Jerry Springer* moment right then and there. He smiled. I did too, but only on the outside. In all honesty, at that moment, I would have loved to have had a *Jerry Springer* moment with my husband right in front of me, letting out all of the anger, frustration and pain from this whole ugly season of life! In reality, it was a good thing he wasn't.

After our initial conversations of disbelief that he hadn't even showed up, we went back to my place and the three of us talked about what we should do now. They suggested we go out and celebrate. We weren't sure what we were celebrating, but going out to eat for lunch seemed like it would be a good distraction from the frustration of the morning. We discussed where we should go for lunch and finally decided on Olive Garden. As we were sitting waiting to be seated, guess who walked in? Yep!! You guessed it!! To all three of our amazement, my husband walked right up to us and began talking to us like we were long lost friends, chatting about everything and nothing, except why he hadn't shown up that morning. You might say the three of us were less than cordial. Thankfully, he had picked up one of our daughters from school to have lunch with or things might have gotten ugly. Seriously, with over 400 restaurants in Green Bay, how in the world did we end up at the same one, at the same time on that day? Had my daughter not been with him, Olive Garden would have most likely been calling the police to break up a real live *Jerry Springer* moment!

Through this whole process, God kept showing me that there are always occasions for me to give in to *Jerry Springer* moments. The greater challenge from Him to me, however, is will I allow the Holy Spirit to work in me and through me *even in* those moments when my flesh wants to lash out? Sometimes it seemed as though the Holy Spirit was asking too much of me. Why can't I act out? Can't I unleash my anger, lash out and go crazy just once? I believed the lie I told myself, that it would certainly make me feel better to let him have it once and for all! And gently I heard the Holy Spirit ask me, "Would it?"

Well, if you're wondering, all of us did stay and have lunch, but not together. Thankfully, we went to one side of the restaurant and they to the other. Yes, and you are right, some of the conversation at our table did evolve around the happenings of this strange day! Here's another example in our world of everyone has rights that reminds us that divorce not only impacts the two people in the marriage, but the children, extended family members and friends of the couple as well.

## Chapter Five

—◆—

# IT'S OVER

*"Should you shield the valleys from the windstorms,*
*you would never see the beauty of their canyons."*
*Elisabeth Kubler-Ross.*

THE FOLLOW-UP APPOINTMENT with the surgeon from the lumpectomy was uneventful. Everything looked normal. I had begun my homeo-pathic treatments and was routinely following up with an oncologist as well to make sure the cancer didn't progress. All in all, my treatment plan seemed to be going well. I thanked God for this surgeon. He was truly a gentle and compassionate soul, always bringing with him a sense of peace and comfort. I honestly believe God handpicked him for me during this season.

For Thanksgiving, since my husband's family lived in town, I vol-unteered to be on-call at the hospital, which allowed the girls the op-portunity to celebrate the holiday with his family. The girls and I would simply celebrate it on another day. Volunteering to be on-call gave me an excuse for not being with my daughters on the holiday when asked by others what my plans were. It also enabled the other chaplains to spend the holiday with their families. I consoled myself with the fact that Christmas was around the corner and the three of us would be going to Michigan to spend it with one of my sisters and her family, which was always a good time. In the interim, there were concerts, plays, and a variety of other holiday activities that seemed to lessen the overriding sadness of sharing the girls, which would inevitably become a permanent part of life sometime in 2003.

2003 did arrive, with the girls and I celebrating the New Year in Michigan. We had a wonderful time with my sister and her family. I wasn't sure what all this year would bring, but, as was my habit, I committed this New Year to the Lord. I was sure that He was able to handle all of it, even if I felt I couldn't. It's funny, for the moment, things didn't seem quite so heavy or sad. Maybe it was because I had just spent some good quality time with some of my family and my girls were there with me in the van. As we were making our way from Southgate, MI back to Wisconsin, we drove through Chicago, a city I truly love! Although the temperature was quite cold that particular day, the sun was shining and the climate in our van was filled with warmth and love as the three of us joined together singing our hearts out to the blaring music of some Contemporary Christian song. Maybe our new normal was going to be okay after all.

The end of January brought with it the trip to Nicaragua. I still couldn't believe how good God was to me in making it possible for me to GO! One positive that came out of the joint custody was that I didn't have to find someone to watch the girls while I was away. My husband was slotted for that time. So, off I went to Nicaragua!

The main purpose of the trip was construction, so there was no lack of opportunity to work out some of my inner frustration through plain 'ole hard work. It was wonderful to be serving from early morning until dinnertime with this team, building a school in an impoverished village. In the evenings, we had services at the local church. And afterwards, it was bedtime. Sleep was a welcome friend who came easily to everyone on the team each evening as we made our way to our beds for the night.

Although this trip was not without tears, it was good to be here. As a matter of fact, it seemed tears were never very far away at all. As paradoxical as it seemed, this trip brought both pain and healing to my heart at the same time! There was a fellow minister from a town only a few hours away from us in the States who was serving as our translator for the trip. He had such compassionate eyes! Like the ones you would have imagined Jesus would have had. He knew some of my story, so it seemed every time he looked at me with his eyes of compassion I would tear up. Jokingly, I told him he wasn't allowed to make direct eye contact with me for the remainder of the trip. We had a few good laughs over that.

My personal highlight of the trip came after one of our evening services. I had gone up to pray for an old woman who needed healing in her body. After I prayed for her, she turned and began to speak directly to me with a spiritual kind of authority. I didn't understand what she was saying, because she spoke Spanish, but I knew it had significance. It felt like she was an Anna. You know, like the one in the Bible who spent her time in the temple and prayed over the Messiah. I felt as though she was giving me some kind of spiritual impartation. Unfortunately, I was unable to get someone to translate what she was saying to me before we left that night.

The next evening, I arranged for my compassionate-eyed friend, our interpreter, to translate our conversation. When asked what she had spoken to me the night before, she simply said she was drawn to me and didn't know what ministry I was involved in but knew there was a calling on my life and for me not to be discouraged. Both that night and the evening prior were treasures from God to me, using this precious woman to give them to me. I thought of how God brought me the 3,576 miles from Green Bay to Nueva Guinea, Nicaragua, not only to help build a school and help minister in the services, but in order to allow this little elderly saint to minister to me! It brought Isaiah 46:11 to mind, "From the east I summon a bird of prey; from a far-off land, a man to fulfill my purpose. What I have said, that I will bring about; what I have planned, that I will do." I love how God does stuff like that. He truly is extravagant in the way He loves His children!

The mission trip wasn't all tears and hard work. There was always time for a practical joke or two. My personal favorite was when I enlisted a younger gal on the trip to join me in having some fun with the others on the team. Because we were the only two single gals on the team, they had given each of us our own small room apart from the others. We all had only cold-water showers. In the afternoon, after a hard day of work, it wasn't so bad. However, on the chilly mornings it was not as appreciated. So, about midway through our trip, we began to talk about the hot showers we had been taking each morning. Of course, we thoroughly embellished how good it felt. It wasn't long before we had every one of the team's attention. Most of the team members asked how we had hot water since they didn't and why hadn't we said something prior to this? Several asked if they could come and take a shower in our shower stall. It wasn't too long before the two of us burst into laughter, giving away our charade. After getting a few hits in the arm, the rest of the team was laughing too. The whole trip ministered to my mind, body and soul and was a welcome relief from life.

Returning home quickly brought me back to reality. The girls, like Ping-Pong balls, traversed back and forth from one house to the other, mostly in one-week-at-a-time increments, or as schedules demanded. Even though this had become normal, my heart still broke for them. Having to pack up some of their stuff every week to go to the other home was their reality. It didn't seem fair that they should have to pay such a high price for their parents' mistakes. I tried to remind myself, in light of our pending divorce, that having both parents involved in their lives was the best-case scenario for them in the long run.

A new final court date had been set. It looked as though, barring another no-show or something unforeseen, March 4, 2003, would be the demise of our now 19 ½ year marriage.

That day finally came. My sister and sister-in-law were unable to make the trip again. Thankfully, a dear friend accompanied me to the final divorce hearing. I must say that her joining me was truly a gift, providing much needed moral support on that occasion. And this time, everyone showed up.

After all of the findings from the judge were read, final arguments given, and the final pronouncements were made, the judge pounded his gavel with an authoritative hit and then uttered words that pierced my heart like a knife, "Divorce has been granted." There it was, just like that.

My mind flashed back to one of the first times we had been in court with the judge. He stated that the plaintiff had filed for divorce stating that our marriage had irreconcilable differences and was irreparable. He asked if I agreed. I responded by telling him that I believe there is no such thing as an irreparable marriage if both parties are willing to work at it and allow God into the equation; therefore, I did not agree. Sadly, one of us had never really allowed God to come into the equation.

I'm not sure what drew me back into the present, but there I was thinking 19 ½ years of marriage had been dissolved with the simple whack of a gavel and the stroke of a pen. What devastated me most was the fact that we had never really worked together toward the possibility of healing and reconciliation, nor had we given God the opportunity to perform a miracle. Part of me was very angry with my now ex-husband for his unwillingness to even try. I was angry too because I was not naïve to the fact that some of the effects of today's decree would linger for a lifetime, especially for the girls. On the other hand, however, part of me sighed with a sense of relief. I looked at my friend and said, "Well, at least it's over." But was it really?

*Chapter Six*

## Surrender to His Will

*"Each divorce is the death of a small civilization."*
*Pat Conroy*

WHEN THE GIRLS came home from school that evening I shared the news with them. Although it didn't come as a surprise to them, it still stung. Like pulling the plug of a loved one that had been on life support, the pronouncement that the divorce was final made our anticipated end become a reality. You see, they, too, had been praying and hoping, against all odds, that something would shift and reconciliation would take place. They, too, wanted a family that was unified, not fragmented. Sadly, nothing shifted. Now that the divorce was official, it was something each of us had to come to terms with in our own way.

For several months prior to the divorce, I had been praying and asking God to show me how to best handle this with my daughters, should it happen. As always, God is faithful to help us through even the most unwanted of times, in a way that brings hope and healing in Him. I told the girls that we would go over to the church after dinner and spend some time praying. They thought it was a good idea as well.

Upon arriving at the church, being an off night, there was no one there but the three of us. I unlocked the main door and we made our way to the sanctuary. I turned on some lights, just enough to help create an atmosphere conducive to prayer, whereby we could each pour out our hearts before God. The three of us gathered at the front. I apologized to them that their dad and I had broken the covenant between us and God that was meant to last a lifetime. I suggested they find a place somewhere in the sanctuary to be alone with God and share whatever was on their heart. I encouraged them to be honest with God and with themselves and reminded them that God was big enough to handle all of the anger, disappointment, pain and whatever else they felt in their hearts.

After some time, I called the girls back up to the front of the sanctuary. I asked if they had anything they wanted to share. We talked for a while and shed some tears. When the conversation seemed to run its course, I looked them both in the eye and again apologized for what their father and I had done. This time, however, I asked them to forgive us while removing the wedding ring from my finger, symbolizing to all of us that the divorce was final. I then reached into my purse and pulled out a small box. I opened it and displayed a beautiful, yet somewhat simple, gold ring with marquis-shaped sapphire stones across the top. I placed it on the finger where my wedding ring had made its home the past 19 ½ years. I told the girls that God had spoken to my heart telling me that He would be our Kinsman Redeemer, as seen in the story of Ruth and Boaz, and that this ring would serve as a reminder of His faithfulness and that we are not on our own. God will watch over and take care of us.

I proceeded to tell them the story of Ruth, one that would take on new meaning for all three of us now. Ruth was a Moabite woman, a foreigner who had married an Israelite. Her husband had died, along with her father-in-law and brother-in-law. She, along with her mother-in-law and sister-in-law had become widows. Her mother-in-law, Naomi, encouraged the two women to return to their homelands with their parents since their spouses had died, which was the custom of the day. After some urging, her sister-in-law chose to go back to her homeland. However, Ruth remained steadfast in her choice to go with her mother-in-law to Israel to find refuge in the God of Israel. The story goes on to tell of how God sovereignly led Ruth to work in a field that belonged to Boaz, which provided for the ladies on multiple levels. Naomi explained to Ruth that he was one of the family's Kinsman Redeemers.

I shared with the girls that a kinsman redeemer was a male relative, in Bible times, who had the privilege or responsibility to act on behalf of a relative who was in trouble, danger or need, giving them authority to vindicate or redeem them. God was reminding all three of us, through this story and symbolized by this ring, that He will redeem our lives from what the enemy had taken and would be our vindicator and our provider. I closed by praying and thanking God for His faithfulness and promised provision for the three of us.

Over the next few months the girls and I gained more stability. The uncertainty of what was going to happen had now been determined. I also had gotten a second resident in our home, so things were picking up financially for us too. God had shown Himself faithful and continued to do so. I will admit, no matter how much time passed, that I never did enjoy seeing my girls pack up and leave to go to their father's, but it had become a regular part of our lives. (Okay, maybe it wasn't so bad when the teenage attitude reared its ugly head from time to time! ☺) We made the most of our time together and I did what I could to keep my schedule as free as possible when the girls were with me. And, on the flip side, when they weren't, I gave any extra time to ministry, picking up more chaplaincy hours or making myself more available at church.

Over the course of several months, I really can't tell you exactly when, God began to speak to my heart. Would I trust Him enough to continue to fight for my marriage in the spiritual realm, in spite of the divorce? As you can imagine, I had more than my share of wrestling matches with God over it. Why would He even ask me to do this? What good would it do or what would it accomplish? I reminded God of His Word which said I was no longer bound. I also told him that this was unfair since I had, at least from my perspective, done everything I could to try and reconcile over the course of the 27 months since our return back to the United States and the divorce. I grappled with it. I cried over it. I fought it. I even yelled at God, telling Him that His request was too demanding.

But God, in His gentle, consistent way, continued to knock on the door of my heart, knowing what would be best for the girls and me in the long run, even if I didn't. Would I be obedient to what He was asking? And, even if I were willing, would it simply bring more pain or a wonderful story of God's redemption in an impossible situation? I had no idea. Redemption sounded very beautiful, although I was under no illusion as to how hard it would actually be to walk out. On the other hand, I was just beginning to come to terms with the divorce and some of the freedom the finality of it brought. I was now free to explore the possibility of another relationship, which, at times, sounded wonderful. Yet, I also knew God could redeem and wanted to redeem our family. The problem remained, were we both willing?

In reality, my ex-husband's actions had not changed. In fact, our lifestyles, which were once quite in sync, had become vastly different. There was nothing in the natural that would pull me towards wanting this relationship restored and obeying what God was asking. However, I had learned that God is faithful and that He can be trusted, even if others or my own emotions can't be. I reminded myself that everything He does is for the good of those who love Him. But the possibility of more pain… no thank you! I thought to myself, God wouldn't ask me to do this for nothing, right? So, in reluctance, despite my best efforts to talk both God and me out of it, I agreed to walk with Him on this new journey of faith. I didn't know exactly what it meant, where it would lead or what the outcome might be, but I knew that trusting *and obeying* God is the *only* way to complete healing and joy. I repeated to myself that God is always good, so this meant He was good *even* in asking me to do this seemingly impossible, unnatural and unwanted task.

I can tell you with certainty that there were moments of vacillation and frustration. God, I want to obey you, but...isn't this asking a bit much? I reminded God that even Jesus stated that there are biblical reasons for divorce! Of course, He already knew that. But I wanted to be free from this whole saga. The divorce had been granted a few months ago. Didn't that give me the right to let go of this entire struggle? I wanted to forget him and move on. To be honest, I wasn't exactly sure what moving on fully involved, but enough people had told me to do it. To my surprise, some of them did it while we were still married! I knew enough to know that wasn't the time or place to quit. I knew that God's Word said what He has brought together man was not to separate. But now, with the divorce final, couldn't I move on? Wasn't I free? I was working toward closing off the emotional part of my heart toward my ex-husband permanently and that was feeling pretty safe and good. After all, hadn't these past two and a half years been painful enough? In reality, I even found peace in knowing that I had truly sought to listen to the Holy Spirit through our entire divorce process and did my best to obey whatever promptings He gave me in working toward the possibility of reconciliation. I had done my part. And, from my perspective, *more* than my part.

So, there it was. God was asking me to remain single and to position myself for the possibility of reconciliation, praying and doing whatever the Spirit led me to do until my ex-husband repented, remarried or died. This meant keeping my heart tender towards God *and him!* After my hurt and disappointment of our failed marriage, keeping my heart tender toward God was a full-time job. Now, add to that, trying to keep my heart tender toward my ex-husband, even when, by doing this, his actions continued to cause me pain?

After many conversations with God, and much struggle, I decided I was in. If He was asking then I was saying yes. After all, how can I call Him Lord if I am not willing to obey and submit to His will? If anything, this process had taught me that God IS faithful and if He was asking me to do this, then there was a good reason behind it, though

I had no clue what. I also knew in my heart that God is faithful and He would bring good fruit from it, no matter the outcome. Although I had no idea what kind of fruit it would be.

A point of clarification: both my ex-husband and I claimed to be believers in Christ during this whole process…beginning to end. That is what made this entire situation impossible for me to walk away from. *IF* we both are believers, then why couldn't there be reconciliation? And why shouldn't there be? Maybe a more clarifying question, why wasn't there reconciliation? If both of us were living lives abandoned to Christ, then obedience to His Word was not an option. After all, Jesus stated that we are His disciples if we obey his teachings. (John 8:31; 14:15-16, 23; I John 2:3; 3:24) His will was clear - a restored, redeemed, marriage for His glory and for the good of our family. And yet, there is the reality of free will. I understood this all too well. God has, since the beginning of time, given us the choice to love Him or to not love Him. Obedience is one of the ways we demonstrate our love to Him and show the world we are His disciples.

# Chapter Seven

A Wedding and a Funeral: New Beginnings

*"I've learned that you cannot make someone love you.*
*All you can do is be someone who can be loved. The rest is up to them."*
*Omer Washington*

ABOUT 8 MONTHS after the divorce it seemed my ex-husband had softened and was, once again, possibly open to the idea of reconciliation. He had surprised me and showed up at the hospital where I was working as a chaplain to have lunch with me. I must admit, it truly was a SURPRISE! You see, I had been working at the hospital for a year and a half and had somehow managed to keep the drama of my personal life out of this arena, with very few knowing what was happening in my personal life, with the exception of one fellow chaplain with whom I had shared my whole story. So, when the secretary of our department paged me and told me that there was a man in our office wanting to have lunch with me and giving me my ex-husband's name, I was stunned! I first reminded myself to breathe and knew there would be questions to be answered later on. Then I shot a prayer upward, "Jesus, help me know what to do."

I managed to find a quiet spot for us to meet where the likelihood of being seen was greatly diminished. My ex-husband told me he wanted to try and reconcile. I will admit, I was skeptical. Why now? What was his angle? I'd been around this bend more than once and wasn't really sure I was ready for it again. Although, I reminded myself, isn't this what I have been praying for? We talked for about 30 minutes, which is all the time I had for lunch. I thanked him for coming and wanting to reconcile and agreed to get back to him soon.

I spent a few days in prayer, asking God to give me wisdom as to how to approach this. After praying I felt like God had given me a game plan. A few days later I met with him again. We talked a lot and he sincerely asked my forgiveness for all he had done to destroy our marriage. I was excited. This was one of the first sincere signs of true repentance I had witnessed since this whole thing happened. We casually talked for a few more minutes. Then I shared with him the 5 things that I felt needed to happen in order for us to move forward: 1) keep this possibility of reconciliation between us, not letting the girls know, until it was clear that things were moving forward; 2) both of us to go to a professional Christian counselor regularly, and, if necessary, submitting to any kind of needed rehab program in order to fully re-establish our marriage; 3) be accountable to someone we both trusted; 4) go to church regularly; 5) and most importantly, not see any other women. He agreed.

I didn't hear too much from him for a week or so, other than an occasional email or quick phone call, mostly related to the girls. I wondered what was really going on and what was going to happen. I continued to pray and submit this to the Lord.

I had invited him to have dinner with the girls and I on a Sunday for something related to one of the girls. He drove into the driveway and I went out on the porch to greet him. We chatted for a few minutes. In our conversation, he told me he had gone to the hospital last night in another town about 45 minutes away with chest pains, which turned out to be panic attacks. As I listened to his story something didn't quite add up, so I asked him how he got back into town. Realizing he was backed into a corner, he reluctantly but casually stated that the woman he had been seeing, but supposedly had quit seeing, picked him up and drove him back home. Needless to say, I was not a happy camper. I told him that was unacceptable, as he had agreed to not seeing any other women. At that point, I stated that he was no longer welcome to dinner.

A few weeks later I received a letter from him in the mail. He again expressed his thanks for my forgiving him and told me of the freedom it gave him. He apologized for hurting my feelings that Sunday, but stated he was unable to fulfill the requirements I had laid out. He continued to say he held me faultless for our divorce and hoped we could remain amicable. Once again, the pain and disappointment of lack of follow through was disheartening to me. I honestly did want reconciliation but knew boundaries had to be set and trust had to be re-established in order for true reconciliation to take place. How can you do that with someone who constantly changes the rules?

This positioning of reconciliation, as I began to call it, went on for years. About another seven years if truth be told. During that time period, God stretched my capacity to love and to feel pain. He asked me to humble myself, many times over, reaching out with new and fresh ways to demonstrate love and a desire to reconcile. During most of this time, God, my ex-husband and I were the only ones who knew what most of these gestures were. Many were just between God and me. I didn't even tell my girls what I was doing in positioning myself for reconciliation because I didn't want them to have false hope.

Sometimes my ex-husband's heart would soften and I would be hopeful he might be willing to change his behavior and work toward reconciliation, but that never did happen. I believed that if both of us allowed God to move and work in our hearts and reconciliation did take place, I could then share all that had been happening behind the scenes with the girls. For the most part, I kept this to myself. I only chose to tell a few of my close, faithful friends what God was speaking to me and how it looked to walk that out. Those few friends were ones whom I knew would encourage me in my pursuit of God at any cost.

Without realizing it at first, I found myself on a journey to a deeper level of obedience to the Master. There were times I still felt God was asking too much. On more than one occasion, some of those who learned of this new journey thought I was crazy. Sometimes I agreed with them and thought I was crazy too! But I continued to choose to obey what I believed God had clearly spoken to my heart. Perfectly? No. But I can honestly say I did it to the best of my ability. I truly had wanted things to work out between my ex-husband and me. I had wanted our relationship to be rebuilt and thrive again and for our family to remain intact. But it didn't. Was there hope for the future? Is that why God was asking me to do this now?

It was about this time I began to understand that, *in reality, this journey I was on was more about the pursuit of a holy God and obeying Him rather than the pursuit of a man for a reconciled marriage.* Yes, I do believe God wanted to reconcile our marriage and family. But, more importantly, He wanted my whole heart, my obedience and my willingness to say yes to whatever He asked of me. The refreshing part of this pilgrimage was that I was *only responsible for me and my responses.* God held my future and already knew the outcome. And He was fully trustworthy! I did not have to fear what He would do, because He *always* has my best interests at heart.

There were times of hope and possibilities as well as disappointment and tears. Other times I experienced complete joy and peace, knowing I had obeyed God's voice, stepped out in another action of faith, providing another opportunity for the possibility of the redemption of our marriage and family. There were times when the gentle voice of God required consistent, steady actions of obedience on my part. Other times, months could go by without me needing to do anything.

After a few years had passed, my girls asked me why I never dated anyone. It was at that point that I explained to them what God had put in my heart. I told them that I was waiting on God to do whatever He wanted to do and trusting Him with the outcome, whatever that may be. I encouraged them not to hold on to some fantasy of their dad and me, but to continue to pray for both of us and to lay their dreams and desires in God's hands.

During this time, I grew to love and trust God more deeply. I grew to rely on His voice and sought His affections more than any other. I reconciled the singleness issue, which brought a certain amount of focus and contentment, trusting God with the outcome. It enabled me to focus totally on being a mom, an adult foster care provider, a hospital chaplain and a missions pastor. Such was the season of life I was in.

At some point in this journey, there was a huge spiritual shift. I began to see this situation as me being bound to Christ in obedience rather than being bound to my ex-husband and his actions or lack thereof. I began to understand a freedom in Christ and in life that I hadn't known before. During this time, I didn't necessarily move on, as many well-meaning friends urged me to do, rather, I moved forward in Christ, in my call and destiny.

Don't get me wrong; there were still times of frustration, loneliness, doubt and disappointment. But, by far, they were outweighed by a sense of satisfaction in knowing I was obeying God and trusting Him with my family, my future and my call. As time continued, I was under no illusion; our marriage possibilities were equivalent to that of a person in a hospital bed being kept alive by machines. Barring an all-out, supernatural miracle, it was dead. That being understood, I continued to move forward in Christ, trusting Him with the possibility of resurrecting our marriage from the dead, if He so chose to do it and we both allowed it.

In May of 2005, I went to my oldest daughter's last high school band concert since she was a senior and would be heading to college in the fall. My daughters had warned me ahead of time that their father was going to be bringing his girlfriend and her daughters. I was glad they had given me time to emotionally prepare. To my surprise, after the concert, my husband and his blonde girlfriend came over. He wanted to introduce me to her. (What?!?! Like I want to be best friends with a woman that had been having an affair with my husband while we were still married?) She extended her hand and casually said, "It's nice to meet you." I looked her squarely in the eyes and retorted quite curtly that I did not feel the same and if her daughters were not in earshot I would have told her exactly how I felt about her, my ex-husband and their rendez vous prior to our divorce. It is a good thing her daughters and ours were within ear shot or I may have said a whole lot more than I should have. I went home and cried that night, telling Jesus everything that was in my heart.

After a few days, the Lord convicted me of my unforgiveness toward the two of them. I tried to reach my ex-husband's girlfriend by phone several times, unsuccessfully. I left a message for her to return my call. After she did not return my call (I can't say that I blamed her!), I wrote her, stating that I chose to forgive her for having an affair with my husband while we were still married and the part it played in destroying our marriage. I also chose to forgive her and my husband for being poor examples to my girls in playing church, yet all the while sleeping together. I continued by asking her to forgive me for the bitterness that I harbored in my heart towards her. I finished by telling her she could call me and talk about this if she wanted to. She never did.

One thing I learned for sure...obedience is definitely hard! At times, seeming almost impossible. But I continued to learn through the process that it produces sweet fruit in the lives of those who dare to trust God with the big picture and do it.

After my girls both graduated from high school, God opened the door for me to be reappointed as a missionary. I had the joy and privilege of leading teams overseas and helping with community transformation projects. This season gave me the joy of traveling and experiencing many new cultures and countries from Africa to Latin America to Asia.

There were opportunities that opened to me because I was single. I began to appreciate these too. I enjoyed being a missionary again and grew in a number of ways; learning some new tools and developing in areas I didn't even know I possessed.

During this season, a well-meaning person in a church gave my business card to another single missionary. He gave me a call to see about the possibility of going out. As we talked he told me that he had divorced his wife because she didn't share his call and passion for ministry. That certainly got my attention! I told him that according to the Bible that was not grounds for a divorce and that he should go and try to reconcile with his wife. He continued to try and rationalize why he felt he was justified in his divorce. I kindly reiterated what I believe God's Word says and, once again, encouraged him to give his ex-wife a call and try to reconcile. I then asked him not to call me again. Needless to say, he didn't.

On the other front, over a period of several years, my ex-husband had gotten engaged twice to the same woman who was at my daughter's band concert. Both times God had directed me to meet with him in person and tell him that he was out of God's will marrying this woman and that God's desire would be for us to recommit ourselves fully to Christ and allow Him to redeem and reconcile our relationship. Since both of us claimed to be believers and claimed to be serving God, reconciliation was what God desired. Both times my ex-husband had broken off the engagement but continued to pursue the relationship with the other woman.

During this season, there was one man that I had met and occasionally had opportunity to run into. He loved Jesus and was involved in missions too. As time passed, it seemed to me that he might be interested in the possibility of a relationship. At very least, I knew that there was the potential for a relationship. I had seen him over the course of about a year and knew he was not one to play with a woman's emotions and did not take deeper relationships lightly. I remember being overseas on a trip when he, to my surprise, Skyped me. He was easy to talk to and we had a lot in common. It was flattering to be contacted by a man whom I respected and was quite sure had intentions of pursuing a relationship. Yet, I knew what God had spoken to my heart. I had to decide if I was going to obey and tell him or continue to toy with the idea of having a relationship. After thinking it over for a few days, I chose the former. I sent him a message explaining to him the marching orders God had given me regarding my ex-husband. To his credit, he told me he understood and never contacted me in this way again. We did, however, run into each other from time to time, but the relationship remained only friends.

In January of 2009, I felt God leading me to do *The Love Dare*, a book which walked me through a 40-day challenge to make the decision to love selflessly, sacrificially and transformationally. I had seen it used and referred to in the movie *Fireproof*. I argued with God, at first. After all, it had been 6 years since our divorce. However, God had still not released me from positioning myself for reconciliation. So, after time and prayer, I decided I had nothing to lose and the possibility of a marriage and an intact family to gain. Having been reappointed as a missionary, I was travelling a lot so it took me a little over 2 months to complete. I was amazed at the transformation that happened in my own heart. I loved that it focused more on my attitudes and responses, yet challenged me to walk out other actions to my ex-husband in faith.

There were definitely times of struggle too. Here is an entry I wrote during the love dare:

"I'm very much desiring a deep relationship. I'm frustrated by the length of our dragging this whole thing out. Eight years of separation and singleness, but over the last year and a half I've longed for relationship. By God's grace and my will, I will choose to be patient and wait for God's best and my ex-husband's choice. Help me God not to be ungrateful for what I have. I choose not to burn for what is forbidden. I will choose to obey you, God."

The actions motivated by the *Love Dare* must have had some impact on my ex-husband. By the time of our oldest daughters' college graduation my ex-husband had told the family that he wanted to reconcile. We gathered in Minneapolis to see her get her diploma. I must admit it was awkward. I tried to celebrate that he was open to reconciliation, yet at the same time deflect the attention it was getting from some of the family members who were at the graduation. My ex-husband and I went for a walk. He, once again, apologized for his actions and stated he truly did want to reconcile. I told him I was glad to hear that and ready to work toward that end also. However, I suggested that we try and focus on our daughter's graduation for the weekend and could move forward with everything after this weekend. I also wanted to see some consistency, any consistency, on follow through of our relationship for both the girls' sake and mine.

Once again, the biggest issue was singleness of heart. He seemed to be unable to focus on just the two of us. There always seemed to be another woman dangling somewhere. My renewed cautious hope once again came to a quick halt.

About a year after that, for a third time, he had proposed to this same woman. I mulled this over with God. I asked Him if I had to go and challenge my ex-husband again to do what was right. And I actually begged God to let him go through with it if my ex-husband was never going to fully commit to reconciliation. This time I felt as though God had given me a release to let him do what he wanted to do. I must admit, by this point, I was relieved. I had learned to continue to move forward in Christ, all the while being cognizant that our divorce was final, yet somehow trusting God for the possibility of the miraculous resurrection of a dead marriage on life support. In all honesty, I was ready for the miracle or the proverbial plug to be pulled.

My ex-husband and his fiancé had set a date. As the day moved closer, I continued to pray for God to work on our hearts, and to bring redemption out of this impossible situation. On the other hand, however, I requested that if our hearts were not malleable enough to let reconciliation happen, then God would let him go through with his remarriage. In anticipation of their wedding, I also asked a few very close friends to come by my home the day after the wedding for a ceremony that would help me bring closure to this very long season.

On the day of their wedding, I had asked my girls to send me a text after the wedding as a simple gesture letting me know if my ex-husband went through with it. About an hour after the wedding was scheduled I received a simple text message saying, "He did it." As I read those three simple words, I had mixed emotions. The reality that this lifeless corpse was now going to be unplugged brought certain sadness to my being. Not that of an overwhelming sadness, rather the death of what was possible, of what could have been. On the other hand, there was relief that this battle, which had lasted almost a decade, was finally over, bringing with it relief and new possibilities.

I spent the remainder of the day in reflection and prayer. I read Scriptures God had given me throughout this journey. I reflected on a few journal entries I had written during this long saga. I also spent some time preparing for the 'funeral,' which would be held tomorrow, representing the death of the possibility of reconciliation and redemption of our marriage. For me, it was the end of any possibility of reconciliation. My ex-husband had remarried and our marriage covenant was irrevocably broken. There was peace in knowing that I had followed the marching orders I believed I had received from the Lord. I could finally lay this to rest, and was more than relieved to be able to do it. I wrote a few thoughts and then gathered a few items that would be buried tomorrow, things that represented different phases, aspects of our marriage and ministry. I slept very well that night.

The next day I went to church as I normally do on a Sunday. I don't really remember what the service was about, but it brought joy and comfort to my being. Afterward, I went home, made the final preparations for the funeral and waited for those chosen few friends who would come and share in this sacred service.

One of the friends that came that day was a missionary colleague who had been my best friend and prayer partner in Madagascar; the one to whom I had joined with in prayer for truth to come out. She just happened to be in the States for about a week, ministering at a close-by congregation and was more than happy to be able share in this funeral ceremony with me. Another gal was one whom I had only known for a few years but we'd become very close. She was in the process of walking a very similar path to the one I was just completing and I had the privilege of mentoring her through it. The final two that would join us were a couple which I had grown to love and respect since moving to Florida for ministry a few years prior.

Each one arrived. We spent a brief time in prayer together. I then shared a very abbreviated story of the journey. Then we took some time for each one of them to write a Scripture or a word on a notecard they felt God had impressed on them to share with me. After each of them had briefly shared, I pulled out the things I had chosen to bury that day, each piece representing something of my ex-husband and my ties together. The first was an old and tattered Bible I had used during our marriage. This represented the breaking of any spiritual ties between us. The second was a beautiful animal print spaghetti strap dress with a cover that I had enjoyed wearing many times since my ex-husband had given it to me as a gift on one of our family vacations. This represented the letting go of any physical ties that might still exist between us. The third was an expensive pair of Escada sunglasses he had bought me several years back. I did not want him clouding my view in any way moving forward. Finally, I put a picture from our wedding day and a prayer card of our family from after the accident. I ripped both in half, strategically severing my ex-husband from me in both pictures. These represented the final breaking of our marriage covenant and a breaking of any ties in ministry that we had together.

I then read out loud to my friends a letter I had written to my ex-husband and his new wife. It stated that I had never seen this as a competition between his new wife and I, rather a walk of obedience and love to God, giving place to the possibility of seeing a miracle in our own marriage and family. I stated that our marriage was irreversibly broken and a new marriage covenant had begun with them. I assured them that I would never do anything to undermine their marriage and that I would encourage our daughters to do the same. I let them know that I prayed their marriage would be successful. And I finished with the verses from Philippians 1:9-11, "…that your love may abound more and more in the knowledge and depth of insight, so that you may be able to discern what is best and may be pure and blameless until the day of Christ, filled with the fruit of righteousness that comes through Jesus Christ—to the glory and praise of God." I placed the letter back in the envelope and would drop it in the mail later that day. Then, together, the five of us prayed and then committed the representations of the remnants of our marriage to the ground.

Ironically, because of where I was living, there wasn't a place to bury them, so I put them down the dumpster chute in my condo complex. I remember chuckling at this thought, an almost comical ending to the honoring of a 27-½ year marriage covenant. As silly as it may seem to some, this was a very meaningful service for me. And to those few close friends who joined me, it was a solemn moment of recognizing the loss of a sacred covenant, yet seeing God's redemption, hope and possibilities for my life and future ahead.

# Chapter Eight

---∾∾---

# THE FRUIT

*"All the art of living lies in the fine mingling of letting go
and holding on."*
*Havelock Ellis*

YOU MAY BE thinking as you read my account that this woman is totally crazy. I wouldn't blame you. You may also be wondering, would God ever ask someone to do this? Or maybe, if God did ask her to do this, why wasn't the marriage restored? These are certainly fair questions. And, to be honest, I've had those same thoughts and asked God the same questions. I even asked God things such as, what was the point of all this? Really, you want me to do that? But as time continued to move forward I began to see the many gifts God had given me through this process and that much of what was changing in the process was me.

First and foremost, keeping my eyes on Jesus and being willing to obey Him, even when I didn't understand, brought me into a much deeper relationship with Him. And even when I felt like I couldn't hear His voice, as I look back I realize He still guided me every step of the way. God opened doors that can only be opened through definitive steps of obedience to what He was asking. His provision and faithfulness during this period of time is unmatched by any other season in my life up to now.

Another huge benefit of keeping my heart open to the possibility of reconciliation kept me from jumping into another relationship prematurely or throwing away my marriage before the divorce was granted. And even after the divorce, as a committed believer, I gave God ample opportunity to reconcile it; therefore, I have peace in my heart that I did everything I could humanly do to try and fight for our marriage. This brought greater wholeness in my own emotionality as well as that of my daughters. And during the whole thing, my energy wasn't spent on proving my worth to myself or others, in attempting to find another relationship. I was able to focus my energy on parenting, work and life right where I was. It also gave me more time, and emotional energy, to invest in others.

This also kept my girls from unnecessary influences in their lives. So often, single parents date and bring significant others in and out of their children's lives, causing needless confusion, stress and sometimes pain to their children, as well as themselves. If you are separated or divorced and have children, be wise in who you bring into your life and theirs.

It seems to be that our culture makes people feel like they aren't significant unless they have a significant other. That is simply not true. Everyone one of us are significant because we are made in the image of Christ. We can be whole and single. You would be wise to put parenting first, creating a stable, safe environment for you and your children to grow and flourish in. Putting your children's welfare above your own will safeguard you from many mistakes.

It may be wise not to even introduce your children to a significant other until you feel confident that the relationship has a strong possibility of becoming a permanent one. This will save all of you from needless hurts and heartaches, and, when you do finally bring a potential relationship into their lives they will take it more seriously. I am confident that God will take care of your needs as you are responsible to steward your children well and take care of their needs.

For me, positioning myself for reconciliation, and continuing to walk that out until my spouse remarried, did several things for me. Because we both professed to be believers, I gave God every possible opportunity, from my end, to redeem our marriage. It is God's greatest desire to redeem and reconcile broken marriages. That is evidenced throughout His Word. Jesus always spoke of a higher love, one that would forgive seventy times seven. And it certainly would have brought glory to Him.

The time I spent in waiting allowed God to bring healing to the many areas of my life that had been affected by the betrayal and divorce. I wanted God to bring wholeness back into every area of my life. And, if I ever remarried, I wanted to be able to offer myself as emotionally whole as humanly possible to my new partner. I wanted to give God the opportunity to heal even the deepest wounds in my life, and to model that to my daughters. I wanted them to experience God's healing in their own lives. I believe that time also gave God ample opportunity to work in both of our hearts. What if there had been true repentance, demonstrated by changed behavior, and a willingness to reconcile on the part of my ex-husband? What if I had jumped into a relationship prematurely, remarried and then he came back to his senses and was open to reconciliation? It would have been too late. For me personally, that would have been difficult to live with. I honestly wanted to give God every possible opportunity from my end for reconciliation so I would have no regrets down the road. I could look deep into the eyes of my daughters and tell them I had done everything humanly possible to reconcile our marriage. And, more importantly, I could stand before God and say the same thing to myself. I knew I had done everything God had asked of me. And with the finality that came through his remarriage, I could sleep in peace, confident I had obeyed God to the best of my ability.

I truly believe, if we will let Him, God will provide everything we need. Too often all of us, myself included, are too quick to create our own answer. After all, though we seldom voice it, we often think we know better than God. At least our actions demonstrate that. And sometimes we, just like Abraham with Ishmael, create our own solution to a situation and end up with a mess that has lasting repercussions for us, our children and grandchildren.

Don't misunderstand me - I believe God is in the redemption business. So, when I sin and repent from a sincere heart and give my mess to Him, He can and will redeem. However, I also understand that even His redemption does not take away some of the consequences of a decision. There is still residue from our divorce. There always will be. But God has redeemed my life, and that of my girls, because we've given the mess back to Him. He is the only one who can truly bring beauty from ashes! However, how much better would it be to seek His will, His guidance in our lives, and to have the kind of joy and peace that only comes through obedience? That, my friend, is the best way.

One of the main 'aha' moments, of how my quest for obedience to God during my divorce process had paid off, came on the day one of my daughters got married. She had a panic attack the morning of her wedding. As we talked about it, I asked her if she was questioning the man she was marrying or the commitment of the marriage itself? After thinking about it for a few moments, she replied that it was the commitment of marriage that concerned her. She then asked me, "Mom, how can I know this will work out for us if it didn't for you and dad?" You see, she knew that her dad and I were committed Christians prior to our marriage. We had fasted and prayed to determine God's will prior to getting married. We had sought God, wise counsel from friends and family, and both shared the same call to missions before we ever walked down the aisle. In light of all of that, my daughter was asking a very sincere, poignant question, having experienced the pain firsthand that came through our divorce.

Sadly, that is one question you really don't want to hear coming from your own child. But here it was and worthy of an honest answer. I remember saying a quick prayer to God, asking Him for the wisdom to answer her. Almost without missing a beat, the Holy Spirit reminded me of something He had dropped into my heart a few weeks prior to this. I was driving in my car, crying, and asking God how I could be a good example to my girls in regard to marriage since ours had failed. He reminded me that I had honored my marriage covenant for 27 ½ years, up to the day that it was irrevocably broken by remarriage. In an instant, I remember the peace and confidence God's words brought to my heart that day. And now those words would be what I offered to my daughter on her own wedding day.

"Honey," I responded, "you've seen two examples lived out before you. One was to walk away from a marriage covenant after 17 ½ years. The other honored a marriage covenant for 27 ½ years. It is up to you to determine which one you will follow. You can't control what anyone else does, but YOU can decide what you will do and choose to keep your eyes on Jesus, following Him by honoring the covenant of marriage you are making today." We prayed together and she, once again, committed their soon to be married relationship to Jesus.

2 Corinthians 1:3-5 says, "Praise be to the God and Father of our Lord Jesus Christ, the Father of compassion and the God of all comfort, who comforts us in all our troubles, so that we can comfort those in any trouble with the comfort we ourselves receive from God. For just as we share abundantly in the sufferings of Christ, so also our comfort abounds through Christ."

Although I would never have chosen this path, it has given me a platform from which I can bring hope and comfort to others who have or are walking down a similar one. It seems there are many today who did not choose divorce or want it, yet they find themselves on this unwanted journey towards it. Because I have walked that way myself, I am able to offer hope, encouragement, and counsel. But, more importantly, direct others to the One who will lead and guide them perfectly according to the path that is right for their particular situation.

Sadly today, many give up on their marriage at the first major disagreement or threat of divorce, long before the gavel ever hits the podium in the court room. Our marriage vows create a marriage covenant, not a contract. The Bible likens marriage to Christ and the Church. Christ gave Himself sacrificially for His Bride, the Church. And God intends that His people keep that covenant before Him. People begin dating other people while they are still married, often being sexually active as well. If you are a Christian this is not acceptable behavior. The Bible clearly teaches celibacy or abstinence outside of marriage. This is for our own good emotionally and physically. When we are sexually active with others we join ourselves spiritually with them. I understand that our culture views this very differently, but the Bible is very clear on this subject.

I don't know where this book finds you today, but I am confident in the grace of Jesus and His blood that covers any sin. It doesn't matter if you have walked through a divorce or if you have dealt with infidelity in marriage, either as the guilty party or the innocent one. Christ has commanded both parties to commit to preserving the covenant of marriage. What does matter is that you are willing to be 100% obedient to what Jesus asks you to do from this point forward. If you are willing to commit your life to Christ as Lord and obey Him in whatever He asks, then, trust me, God can and will do amazing things!! No matter the situation or the other person's decision(s), God can and does still redeem. He is faithful!

If you find yourself in a struggling marriage, I challenge you to seek God and ask Him to redeem your marriage. Ask Him to show you the path that He has for you. Read His Word, the Bible. Seek godly counsel. Pray. And listen. I believe if you will do that God will speak to you and guide you into the path that is right for you and your situation. Remember to line everything up with God's Word. His Word will never lead you astray.

No matter how broken your past or present may seem, God is faithful. He is the divine Fixer Upper! The singing group, Point of

Grace, wrote a song called *Heal the Wound*. It ministered to me many times during my years of waiting on God and continually laying before Him my mess. The song speaks to the fact that our scars are reminders of how merciful God is to us and what He has brought us through. I can tell you confidently that if you will give Him all of your brokenness, shame, bitterness and anger, He will make something beautiful out of it. Most likely, it will not happen overnight, but, if you continue to take His hand, it will happen in His timing and His way. And you can trust me when I say it will be worth it all in the end!

# Epilogue

# Beauty From Ashes

*"It is amazing what God can do with a broken heart,*
*if He gets all the pieces."*
*Samuel Chadwick*

## Isaiah 61:1-4

"The Spirit of the sovereign Lord is on me, because the Lord has anointed me to proclaim good news to the poor. He has sent me to bind up the brokenhearted, to proclaim freedom for the captives and release from darkness for the prisoners, to proclaim the year of the Lord's favor and the day of vengeance of our God, to comfort all who mourn, and provide for those who grieve in Zion—to bestow on them a crown of beauty instead of ashes, the oil of joy instead of mourning, and a garment of praise instead of a spirit of despair. They will be called oaks of righteousness, a planting of the Lord for the display of His splendor."

At the time of the writing of this book, it has been 17 years since my ex-husband and I separated and 15 years since our divorce was final.

I have learned, through my struggles, that it is only by His grace, and my partnership with it, that I can choose to do what is right. And, the more I do it, the easier it gets. Don't get me wrong, it is rarely easy, but the choice to choose it becomes easier. Why? Because of the beautiful fruit it produces in our lives. That is where the treasure comes in. That is what makes the initial painful choice of obedience possible...knowing that God's principles are true and He is faithful. He will do what He says He will do. He does bring beauty from ashes and does give the oil of joy for mourning. But, more importantly, He will walk with you, guide you, and even carry you, every painful step of the way...if you'll let Him.

There have been many positive benefits that came from that season of obedience, both in my life and in that of my daughters also. Truly, I can tell you that Jesus has redeemed my life in every way. First of all, I am cancer free. Since the occurrence in 2002, I have not had a reoccurrence. For that, I thank Jesus!

Both of my daughters are married and have blessed me with 5 precious grandchildren. They and their husbands are following Jesus and choosing to work through challenges that arise in life instead of walking away from them. And they are reaping the benefits of their own determination to walk in obedience to God. Another reason I am truly grateful.

After almost 15 years of being single, God brought a wonderful man into my life. He truly is my surprise package from Jesus! He was a pastor whom I had known from our circle of ministry for about 20 years prior to our getting together. He had been married 41 years to his first wife, before she died unexpectedly in 2014. At the end of April 2015, we began getting to know each other on a more personal level through Facebook messenger. We spent hours instant messaging back and forth, asking questions and responding, in order to find out likes, dislikes, philosophy of ministry, long-term goals, dreams, finances, etc. You name it...most likely one of us asked it! After meeting each other's adult children and gaining their approval for our relationship, we married in September of the same year. At the writing of this book, we've been married more than 2 ½ years! He always teases that we have to live long enough to at least make it to 41 years so we can tie his first marriage. Since neither of us are spring chickens, I guess we'll have to leave the longevity of our marriage up to Jesus!

When we married, I was able to fully commit and engage with him, without the feelings of guilt, shame or uncertainty regarding my first marriage. I didn't enter my second marriage half-heartedly or broken. Because of God's grace, I gave myself to him wholly (or as whole as any of us can be). I didn't second-guess if I had done enough to try and make my first marriage work. I had the confidence that came from obedience, knowing I had done everything humanly possible to try and make my first marriage work, so I knew I could give myself till death parts us for the second. I understood the meaning of covenant and the cost of carrying that out before God from my first marriage. Conversely, I also know the beauty that comes from a covenant honored by two people who guard it as sacred and work toward keeping and building that relationship rightly before God.

Another bonus was that my daughters were ready to accept him too. I hadn't dated at all prior to him, so when I told them I was dating him they knew it had to be something serious. They also knew there must be something pretty special about him too. And, they were right!! He is a gem! God has blessed me with a godly man with whom to share life. And by bringing us together, He gave me two new sons (in addition to my sons-in-law) and two more grandchildren. By bringing us together, God also birthed another ministry in which the two of us are both involved, using both of our combined ministry experiences. It has been a fun 3-year journey so far and, should the Lord tarry, we look forward to many more years together!

Don't misunderstand me. I am not saying there are no scars or baggage from my journey. There remains the inconvenience, and sometimes tension that is caused by holidays and other special moments or events in life, when my daughters, for whatever reason have to choose one situation over another. As long as both my ex-husband and I remain alive, there will remain an extra pull on my daughters and their families, some of which could have been eliminated if our marriage had survived. But we have all learned to make the most of our situation, accepting it for what it is. And God gives grace and strength as we look to Him to cover the challenges. We have also chosen to see the scars that remain for what they truly are, a reminder of His mercy and grace that brought us out of that difficult season and into another place.

Please don't think you will ever totally escape pain or disappointment or trials. That simply is not true. We live in a sinful world. But only God can, and DOES, bring redemption, restoration and resolution to one's soul, even when everything looks totally hopeless and impossible. I promise you, if you choose the path of obedience to Jesus, it will be worth it and there will be beauty in the end. That beauty, however, may be different than you expected, but nonetheless glorious.

Yes, this journey of obeying Jesus has been worth it. I am living life, growing as an individual and a married woman, but most importantly as a follower of Christ. I continue to have opportunities to make the choice to obey Jesus every day in some way or another. But I have learned that obedience IS worth it! And I promise you, if you will get out of your comfort zone and say yes to Jesus, obeying Him and allowing Him to guide your every step, you too will say that obedience is worth it!

That being said, I am more convinced than ever that God's way is the best way...*especially* when it looks contrary to that in reality. And I truly believe that obedience to Jesus Christ is the only path that brings true and lasting joy, peace and satisfaction, especially in the midst of less than ideal circumstances. I can promise you, if you choose the path of obedience to Jesus, it will be worth it and you will find beauty in the end.

OBEDIENCE: IS IT WORTH IT?

You may be thinking it is too late for you because of choices you've made in the past. No matter where you are or what you've done, God is a redeemer. If you are willing to give Him all of your pieces He can take your ashes and make something beautiful out of them. Only He can. But I will warn you, true beauty is costly, but it is also more precious. And the lone path to getting there is obedience. Trust me when I say that obedience to Jesus is worth it!

# Points of Clarification

**POSITIONED for RECONCILIATION:**

This is a phrase I coined during my years of waiting. It means to keep your heart in a position of surrender and submission to God, in that you are willing to obey and do anything God asks of you. It is seeking Him above everyone and everything else in your life, all the while keeping your heart open to the possibility of the reconciliation of your marriage, should your spouse repent, which will be evidenced by changed behavior. It means giving up to God, over and over again, your pain, shame, anger, bitterness and worry, as well as your will, your rights and your desires to do whatever God is asking of you. It is a place of surrender to God, whereby you are looking to Him as your Source for direction, guidance, stability and peace. You are following His lead, in relation to your spouse, not the demands of your spouse or others. It is a place of allowing yourself to keep an emotionally healthy distance from your spouse, if needed, without shutting the door to the possibility of reconciliation until God directs you to do so. It is not riding their rollercoaster, as I referred to earlier.

This is not an easy place to get to, but once you do, for the most part, it is a place of peace, quiet confidence and trust that God truly does have your best interest in mind (and if applicable, that of your children) as you wait on Him. It is important to understand that it can also be a place where others may misunderstand you. That is why it is so important to read God's Word, listen to the promptings of the Holy Spirit and seek godly counsel from those you trust. This may be a time when you need to limit the amount of people that you give the right to speak into every area of your life. For example, during this season in my life, I had limited the number of people I shared everything with to two girlfriends who had proven themselves to be trustworthy, godly friends prior to this time. With these two chosen confidants I shared my struggles, fears, decisions, etc. These two had the right to ask me about anything to help keep me accountable. At times, they challenged me about my attitude or actions. Other times they asked for clarification as to why I thought God was leading me this way or that, etc. God often used them to bring confirmation to me when He was speaking to my heart or clarity when I was unsure.

I also had two male pastor friends, who were like brothers to me. I would bounce off of them ideas, thoughts, etc. that needed a male perspective. In order to guard from any unhealthy transference of emotion on either part, I always made their wives aware of when I had talked to them and limited the scope of our conversation to appropriate topics, keeping our relationship healthy, pure and Christlike. While I certainly shared some things with other people besides these four, I limited what I shared in order to protect others from developing offenses that they may take up on my behalf in the event that my ex-husband and I ever reconciled. This also guarded me from getting too many opinions regarding something I felt God was speaking to me about, possibly adding confusion.

I honestly believe that if more people would hit the pause button, position themselves for reconciliation and seek God on behalf of their marriage, we would see more marriages and families restored. Not only would marriages be restored, but they would be healthier and stronger than before. Sadly, most of us don't give God the opportunity to restore our marriages, partly because there is a lack of godly counsel in our culture and, sadly, within the Church body as well. We've accepted the lie that it is our right to be happy. We often hate to see someone hurt and therefore counsel that they should simply move on. It is important to remember that Jesus never came to make us happy, rather He came to make us holy, which will eventually make us whole and bring true joy in our lives.

## WILL YOU???

If you find yourself in a situation where your marriage is crumbling, and is in need of a miracle, will you give God the opportunity to do something? In you? And possibly even in your marriage? Seek Him. Read His Word and **obey**. If you are willing to do that, only heaven knows what beauty lies within your ashes and your situation.

## TAKING A 'BROTHER' TO COURT:

The Apostle Paul, in I Corinthians 8, talks about taking a fellow believer to court. I have a few things to say in this regard. First of all, I believed this word and did not take anyone to court. However, in the end, I was taken to court. I wanted to reconcile the marriage and avoid the court scene entirely. However, that did not happen. Having been served papers, I had two choices. The first would have been to ignore it and allow my now ex-husband to determine how everything was going to turn out. The second choice was to find someone to represent me, protect me and help get what was just, given our judicial system. Allowing my ex-spouse to determine the outcome of child custody, division of assets and debts, alimony, etc., most likely, would not have been in my or the girls' best interests, personally or financially. All of these are serious matters with lasting consequences that need to be evaluated by someone who understands the law and who is not emotionally tied to your situation. That being said, it is important to weigh your own motives and pray and ask God to guide you. I don't believe it is Christian character to go for the jugular, and try to take your former spouse for every penny you can get. Not that I didn't ever think about doing that at some point; however, I chose not to. Even in this I tried to honor the Lord with my actions, wanting only what was equitable and just for the girls and me in light of our circumstances and the judicial system.

Scripture does warn us to beware of taking another believer to court. (I Corinthians 6:1) It is also necessary for us, as believers, to be wise if you are taken to court. Pray and ask Jesus to give you wisdom in regard to your specific situation. Pray and ask God to direct you to the right person to represent you, if necessary. *If* both parties are believers, then see if there is some way it can be worked out with godly leadership. Sadly, we have lost much of the ability for a mediator to help us in our sue-happy era and culture of independence in which we find ourselves today. It is important for you to seek God and measure your own actions against the Bible and what it has to say. Remember to work on keeping your own heart right in every situation, doing your best to allow the fruit of the Spirit to be evident in your life. The fruit of the Spirit in the life of the other party (and your own) will give you a good idea of whether or not you are really dealing with a committed believer or someone who simply claims to be, seeking their own ends. Seek godly, biblical guidance from those you trust and know to be living a biblical lifestyle.

There may be times when it is necessary for the believer to file a lawsuit. This should be the exception and not the rule. Again, earnestly seek God for wisdom. God may direct you to separate for a time, giving your spouse a little tough love in hopes to lead them to repentance or to protect you and your children from physical or emotional abuse. Seek godly counsel. Read the Bible to determine what God has to say about your situation. God may direct you to file a legal separation, which can help protect you to some degree financially, while still guarding the marriage. (Note: not all States honor a legal separation.)

I realize there are more situations out there than I can imagine. And you may be asking, what about my particular situation? Is it right to…? All I know is that, if you are honestly willing to let God guide you, He will be faithful to direct you through His Word and godly counsel for your specific situation. And if you will obey the promptings of the Holy Spirit, no matter what your partner does, God will redeem your situation and you will reap the benefits of obedience.

## NOT RECONCILIATION AT ANY COST.

It is also important to note that when I am talking about reconciliation, it is not reconciliation at any cost. *True repentance will result in changed behavior.* If there isn't changed behavior, most likely there isn't true repentance. It would be a very rare instance that God would ask someone to stay in a relationship where a spouse is continually unfaithful, while professing his love to you. Nor would it be wise to stay in a situation where you or your children's lives are in danger. Again, seek God. He will direct you as to what you should do and then do it. He is more than faithful to guide you in the midst of your situation and to see you through it. And, if you are willing to give God all of your pieces, the good, the bad and the ugly, there will be beauty on the other side of it.

## SIMPLE GUIDELINES OF HOW
## TO DETERMINE GOD'S WILL.

Determining God's will may sometimes be difficult. However, with that in mind, here are a few simple guidelines that may help you. First and foremost, what you sense God is speaking to you must line up with the Word of God, the Bible. God will never contradict His Word, so you can always look here first to see what God has to say to you about your particular situation. Here are a few passages about divorce which may help you: Malachi 2:13-16, I Corinthians 7:10-16,

Matthew 5:31-32; 19:3-12, Mark 10:2-12, Luke 16:18, Romans 7:2-3, Hebrews 13:4. Second, seek godly counsel from trusted pastors and friends. Share your heart with them and then listen to what they have to say.

Third, take time to pray about it. Listen to the Holy Spirit. The Bible tells us that the Spirit will guide us into all truth. Pray and ask Him to guide and direct you. Submit your own personal will and agenda over to God. Give Him control of your situation and permission to move according to His divine purpose and plan. We are often clouded by our own circumstances, feelings, and emotions and therefore need to submit them to God. Fourth, look at your circumstances. This can be a bit trickier, because sometimes God will direct in a way that may initially seem counterintuitive; however, circumstances can sometimes help determine what God is saying to you...especially if they are out of your control.

These simple ideas are certainly not exhaustive, but they may serve to help you as you seek God to determine His will for you. Remember, God delights in the fact that you want to know His will. He is a good Father and will guide you. Commit your ways to the Lord and He will direct your path. (Proverbs 3:5-6, 16:3, Psalm 37:5-6)

CPSIA information can be obtained
at www.ICGtesting.com
Printed in the USA
FFOW02n0116080618
47083541-49509FF